Lindsay Clandfield & Adrian Tennant

Straightforward

Beginner Workbook

MACMILLAN

Macmillan Education
4 Crinan Street, London N1 9XW
A division of Springer Nature Ltd

Companies and representatives throughout the world

ISBN 978-0-230-42299-5 Workbook
ISBN 978-0-230-42298-8 Workbook plus Answer Key
ISBN 978-0-230-42297-1 Workbook plus Answer Key and Workbook Audio CD
ISBN 978-0-230-42296-4 Workbook and Workbook Audio CD

This edition published 2013
First edition published 2007

This edition designed by eMC Design Limited
Original design by Oliver Design
Illustrated by Fred Blunt pp6, 14, 23, 49, 56; Anne Cakebread pp5, 19, 21, 31, 39, 42; Mark Duffin p23; Joanna Kerr pp9, 11, 13, 18, 22, 24, 26, 29, 32, 41, 47, 52, Peter Lubach pp27, 28, 44, 53; Julian Mosedale pp8, 12, 15, 46; Mark Ruffle pp9, 11, 19, 20, 26, 27, 28, 29, 33, 44
Cover design by eMC Design Limited
Cover photograph by Getty Images/Doug Chinnery (main); Alamy/Robert Harding Picture Library Ltd; Corbis/Roger Tidman; Corbis/Lois Ellen Frank; Corbis/Gerolf Kalt; Alamy/Images & Stories.
Picture research by Sally Cole

Authors' acknowledgements
Lindsay would like to thank Philip Kerr for believing in him at the very beginning. As always, a great thank you must go to my wife Sofia and my children Lucas and Marcos for all their support.

Adrian would like to thank his wife, Agi and daughter, Aliz for the support they've given him, and Molly (the dog) for taking him on walks to give time and space to think. He'd also like to thank Lindsay for making writing together such a pleasure.
The publishers would like to thank all the teachers from around the world who provided invaluable comments, suggestions and feedback on the first edition.

The publishers would also like to thank the following people for their help and contribution to the second edition:
Tatiana Baytimerova (Russia), Lenka Boehmová (Czech Republic), Dr. Manuel Padilla Cruz (Spain), Svetlana Elchaninova (Russia), Jennifer Díaz Green (Dublin), Elena Mokeeva (Romania), Lynn Thomson (freelance editor), Amany Shawkey (Macmillan Egypt), Maria Teresa Rius Villaplana (Spain), Natalia Vorobyeva (Russia).

The author(s) and publishers are grateful for permission to reprint the following copyright material:
Pg 66: Story from Macmillan Reader series 'The Black Tulip', copyright © Florence Bell 1998, 2002 & 2005, reprinted by permission of Macmillan Education.

The authors and publishers would like to thank the following for permission to reproduce their photographs:
AFP p48; **Alamy**/Alaska Stock p43(cr), Alamy/Bon Appetit p10(bl), Alamy/J.Arnold Images Ltd p13(B), Alamy/G.Avila p25(l), Alamy/J. Bedford Photography p31(tcr), Alamy/Corbis Cusp p30(l), Alamy/P. Doyle p34(l), Alamy/D.Makabaw p32(c), Alamy/Motoring Picture Library p17(cl), Alamy/P.Noyce p17(tc), Alamy/R.Noyes p50, Alamy/Photo Alto p22(c), Alamy/Rubberball p13(A), Alamy/A.Segre p13(B), Alamy/Image Source p21(D), Alamy/Simple Signs p45(bl), Alamy/J.Sullivan p62, Alamy/TravelStock Collection/H.Sykes p6(2), Alamy/The Photolibrary Wales p17(tr), Alamy/J.Weisberg p60; **Archive Holdings Inc** p17(bl);**Bananastock** p13(B); **Blend Images** p25(c); **Corbis** p41(c), Corbis/Axiom Photographic/Design Pics p54, Corbis/Blend Images pp10(cr), 21(c), 43(tr), Corbis/Hulton Deutsch Collection p41(tl), Corbis/Envision p10(tc), Corbis/Paquet/EPA p13(A), Corbis/D.Sailors p31(tcl), Corbis/Image Source pp13(B), 18(1), Corbis/C.Rehm/Westend61 p21(A); **DigitalStock**/Corbis p6(4); **Eyewire** p13(A); **Film Magic** p16(1); **Hulton Archive** p41(cr); **Image Source** pp13(A), 15(cl), 31(tl), 61(l); **Mercedes Benz UK Ltd** p6(1); **Photodisc** p51(l);**Rex Feaures**/Moviestore Collection pp35(tl), 35(bl); **Stone** pp4(tr), 30(c); **Superstock**/Blend Images p55, Superstock/M.Ford p37(l), Superstock/Age Fotostock p6(3), Superstock/Robert Harding Picture Library p57(cr), Superstock/Hemis.fr p61(tr), Superstock/G.Lacz Images p10(cl), Superstock/P.Phipp/Travelshots p31(bl), Superstock/Pixtal p40, Superstock/L.Radeka p61(cr), Superstock/Somos p59, Superstock/Travel Library Ltd p57(tr); **Taxi** pp17(cr), 21(B); **The Fitzwilliam Museum,Cambridge** p51(r); **Workbook Stock** p4(tl).

Printed and bound in Great Britain

2019
10 9 8

Contents

Writing

1A My name

Greetings (1)

1 Rearrange the letters to make words.

1 elohl *hello*
2 ih ______________
3 dogobey ______________
4 ybe ______________

To be (1)

2 Rewrite the sentences using contractions.

1 My name is Bond.
My name's Bond.
2 What is your name?
______________________________?
3 I am Olga.
______________________________.
4 My name is Hamed.
______________________________.
5 I am Mr Gomez.
______________________________.

Asking & saying names

3 Rearrange the words to make sentences or questions.

1 your name What's
What's your name?
2 Orion My name is .
____
3 am I Kim .
____
4 Daniel my is name Hi, .
____

4 Complete the dialogue with the words and phrases from the box.

Hi	your name	I'm	My name

A: Hello. (1) ______________ Jack.
B: (2) ______________, Jack.
A: What's (3) ______________?
B: (4) ______________'s Brian.

Translation

5 Translate the words and sentences into your language.

1 Hello.
______________________________.
2 Goodbye.
______________________________.
3 My name's …
______________________________.
4 I'm …
______________________________.
5 What's your name?
______________________________?

1B | My country

ASKING & SAYING WHERE YOU'RE FROM

1 Look at the picture above and make sentences using the prompts.

1 They / Russia

They're from Russia.

2 She / Germany

____.

3 They / Britain

____.

4 They / the US

____.

5 He / Brazil

____.

6 She / Italy

____.

7 We / China

____.

TO BE (2) (*MY, HIS, HER*)

2 Correct one mistake in each sentence.

1 ~~*What*~~ *What's your name?*

2 She are from Russia.

3 Where you are from?

4 I from Berlin.

5 His name is Emily.

6 Nice meet you, Emily.

CITIES & COUNTRIES

3 Complete the sentences with the cities from the box.

Rome	~~Beijing~~	Rio de Janeiro	Moscow
New York	Frankfurt		

1 *Beijing* is the capital of China.

2 ____________ is the capital of Russia.

3 ____________ is in Brazil.

4 ____________ is in the US.

5 ____________ is in Germany.

6 ____________ is the capital of Italy.

GREETINGS (2)

4 Put the sentences in the correct order to make a dialogue.

- [ ] Nice to meet you, too.
- [1] Hello. I'm Max.
- [ ] Nice to meet you.
- [ ] Hello, Max. My name's Victoria.

5 **01** Listen to the recording to check your answers.

LISTENING

6 **02** Listen to the rest of the dialogue. Answer the questions.

1 Where's he from?

____.

2 Where's she from?

____.

1c | My number

Greetings (3)

1 Complete the dialogue with the words from the box.

you	fine	I'm	are	thanks

A: Hi, Jack. How (1) ________ (2) ________?

B: (3) ________ (4) ________, thanks. And you?

A: Fine, (5) ________.

Numbers 1–10

2 Look at the alphabetti-spaghetti and find ten numbers.

seventwofiveoneeightninethreetenfoursix

3 Write the numbers in words.

1	________	*6*	________
2	________	*7*	________
3	________	*8*	________
4	________	*9*	________
5	________	*10*	________

It

4 Complete the sentences with *he* or *it*.

1 _____'s from Germany.

2 _____'s from China.

3 _____'s in New York.

4 _____'s in India.

Dictation

5 **03** Write the phone numbers that you hear.

1 ________________________________

2 ________________________________

3 ________________________________

4 ________________________________

1 Test yourself

Functional language

1 Rearrange the words to make sentences or questions.

1 meet you Nice to .

____

2 you are How ?

____

3 name your What's ?

____

4 This Philip is .

____

5 your number phone What's ?

____

/5

2 Match the sentences or questions 1–5 from exercise 1 to the phrases a–e.

☐ a Nice to meet you, too.
☐ b Nice to meet you, Philip.
☐ c My name's Margaret.
☐ d It's 622 4031.
☐ e Fine, thanks.

/5

Grammar

3 Complete the sentences with *is*, *am* or *are*.

1 What ______ your phone number?
2 Her name ______ Stefi.
3 I ______ from England.
4 Where ______ you from?
5 He ______ from Moscow.

/5

4 Tick (✓) the correct sentence, a or b.

1 a) His name is Ronnie. ____
b) He name is Ronnie. ____
2 a) He is from Brazil. ____
b) I is from Brazil. ____
3 a) They are David and Michael. ____
b) They is David and Michael. ____
4 a) We am in Paris. ____
b) We are in Paris. ____
5 a) I am Sam. ____
b) I are Sam. ____

/5

Vocabulary

5 Write the missing numbers.

one
two
(1) __________
four
(2) __________
(3) __________
seven
(4) __________
nine
(5) __________

/5

Total: /25

2A | Hotel lobby

Spelling names

1 Look at the pictures and complete the sentences with the phrases from the box.

do you spell	Excuse me	Thank you	your name

A ☐ **B** ☐ **C** *1* **D** ☐

2 Look at the pictures in exercise 1 and put the dialogue in the correct order.

Numbers 11–20

3 Write numbers from the letters.

t e w v l e

1 *twelve*

n s e e v e t n e

2 ________

n n i e n e t e

3 ________

n f o e u e t r

4 ________

n f i e f e t

5 ________

n e l e e v

6 ________

4 Match the words 1–6 from exercise 3 to the numbers a–f.

a 11 ________

b 12 ________

c 14 ________

d 15 ________

e 17 ________

f 19 ________

Listening

5 **04** Write the names that you hear.

1 ________

2 ________

3 ________

4 ________

2B | Hotel room

Common objects

1 Rearrange the letters to make words.

1 nep ____________
2 tooboken ____________
3 nohepelet ____________
4 adiro ____________
5 eky ____________

2 Match the words 1–5 from exercise 1 to the objects A–E.

A ☐

B ☐

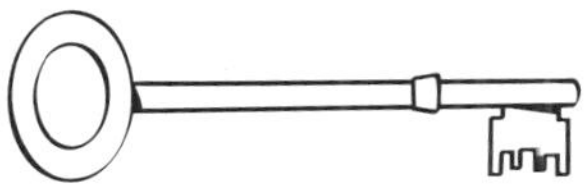

C ☐

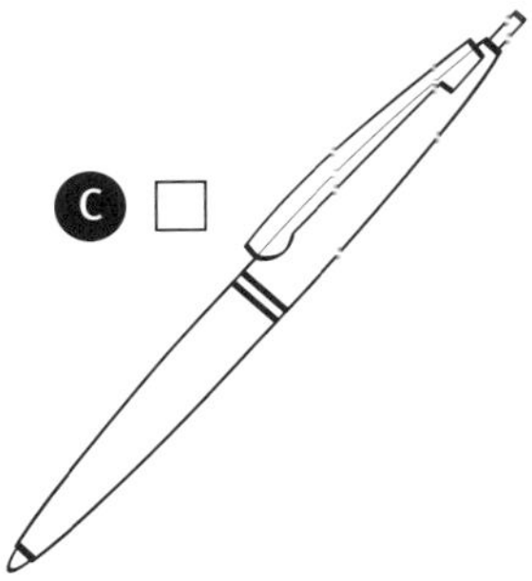

D ☐

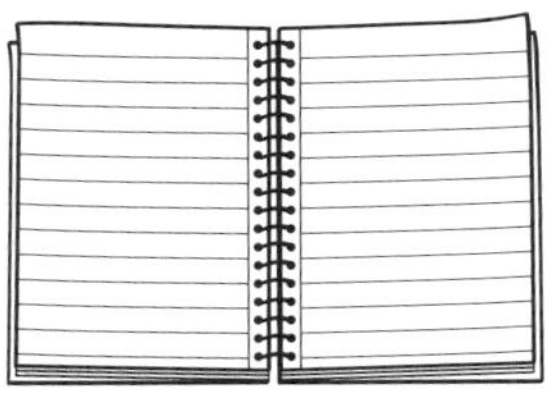

E ☐

This/that/here/there

3 Look at the pictures and tick (✓) the correct sentence, a or b.

1 a) This is a radio. ____
b) That's a radio. ____

2 a) This is a chair. ____
b) That's a chair. ____

3 a) Is this your pen? ____
b) Is that your pen? ____

4 a) That's the man, there! ____
b) This is the man, here! ____

Translation

4 Translate the sentences into your language.

1 What's that?
________________________________?

2 I don't know.
________________________________.

3 This is a television.
________________________________.

4 It's a pen.
________________________________.

5 Your books are here.
________________________________.

2c | Hotel café

Food & drink

1 Complete the table with the words from the box.

apple juice coffee ~~croissant~~ tuna sandwich
mineral water omelette tea

food	drink
croissant	

Plurals, *a/an*

2 Choose the correct word or phrase to complete the sentences.

1 I'd like *a* / *an* tea, please.
2 Would you like *a* / *an* omelette?
3 An *apple juice* / *apple juices*, please.
4 *A* / *An* croissant and *a* / *an* coffee, please.
5 Two *coffees* / *coffee*, please.
6 I'd like a tuna *sandwich* / *sandwiches* and two *tea* / *teas*.

In a café

3 Put the sentences in the correct order to make a dialogue.

☐ Cheese, please.
☐ Would you like cheese or tuna?
☐ Here you are.
☐ I'd like an omelette, please.

Dictation

4 **05** Write the sentences that you hear.

1 ______________________________.
2 ______________________________.
3 ______________________________?
4 ______________________________.

2 | Test yourself

Vocabulary

1 Write the missing numbers.

eleven, (1) ____________, (2) ____________, fourteen, (3) ____________, (4) ____________, seventeen, (5) ____________, nineteen, (6) ____________

/6

2 Look at the pictures and complete the sentences.

1 This is a ____________. 2 This is a ____________.

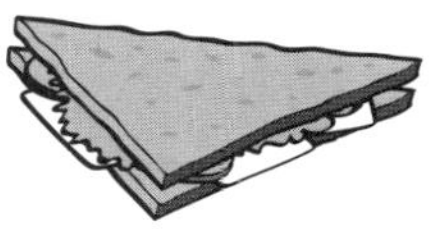

3 This is a ____________. 4 This is a ____________.

/4

Grammar

3 Choose the correct word to complete the dialogues.

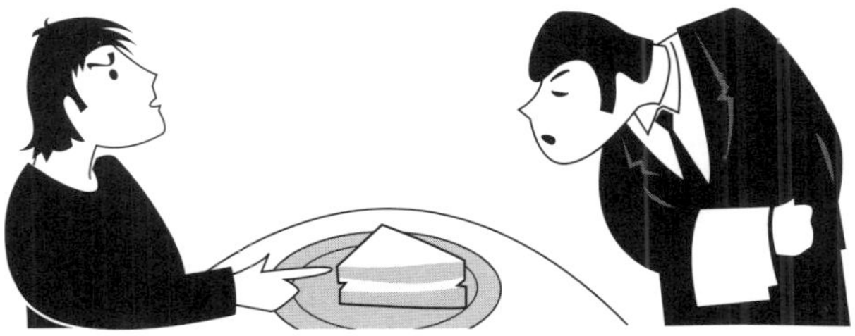

A: Excuse me! What's (1) *this* / *that*?
B: It's (2) *a* / *an* cheese sandwich.

C: Is (3) *this* / *that* the hotel?
D: Where?
C: (4) *Here* / *There*.

E: I'd like (5) *a* / *an* orange juice, please.

/5

Functional language

4 Rearrange the words to make sentences and questions.

1 name your What's ?

____

2 do How your name spell you ?

____

3 a please like croissant I'd .

____

4 still you or sparkling Would like ?

____

5 Would you a coffee like ?

____

/5

Listening

5 **06** Listen and complete the dialogue.

Customer: Excuse me. I'd like (1) _______ _______, please.

Waitress: (2) _______ _______ _______ black or white?

Customer: Black, (3) _______.

Waitress: (4) _______ _______ are.

Customer: (5) _______ you.

/5

Total: /25

1 & 2 | Reading

1 Read the dialogue and put the pictures in the correct order.

Jack and Emily

A ☐

B ☐

C ☐

D ☐

E ☐

F ☐

G ☐

2 Read *Jack and Emily* again and complete the sentences.

1 Her name is ____________.
2 His name is ____________.
3 She's from ____________.
4 He's from ____________.
5 They are from ____________.

READ & LISTEN

3 **07** Listen to Reading 1 & 2 *Jack and Emily* on the CD and read the dialogue again.

3A | International workers

Jobs

1 Match the pictures A–E to the jobs 1–5.

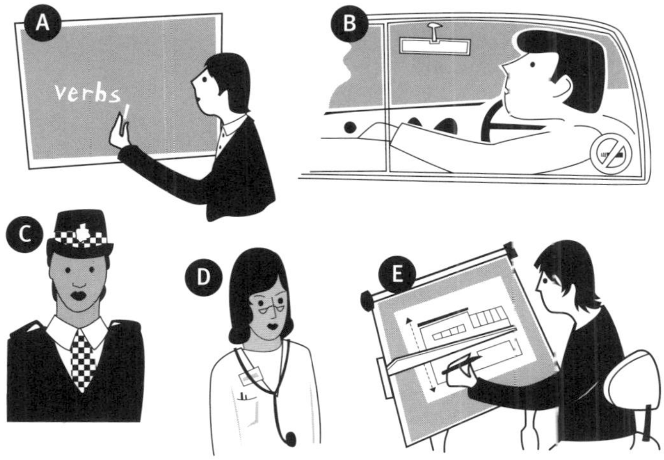

1 ☐ taxi driver
2 ☐ teacher
3 ☐ doctor
4 ☐ police officer
5 ☐ architect

2 Tick (✓) the correct sentence, a or b.

1 a) She's a architect. ____
  b) She's an architect. ____
2 a) He's a diplomat. ____
  b) He's an diplomat. ____
3 a) I'm a police officer. ____
  b) I'm an police officer. ____
4 a) Phil's a teacher. ____
  b) Phil's an teacher. ____

To be (affirmative)

3 Choose the correct word to complete the sentences.

1 She *am* / *are* / *is* a doctor.
2 I *am* / *are* / *is* from Sydney, Australia.
3 We *am* / *are* / *is* students.
4 What *am* / *are* / *is* your job?
5 Sabrina *am* / *are* / *is* a teacher.

Asking about jobs

4 Rearrange the words to make questions and sentences.

1 your What's job ?

______________________________?

2 police officer a I'm .

______________________________.

3 do do What you ?

____

4 a student I'm .

____

Listening

5 **08** Tick (✓) the correct photo, A or B.

1 A ____
  B ____

2 A ____
  B ____

3 A ____
  B ____

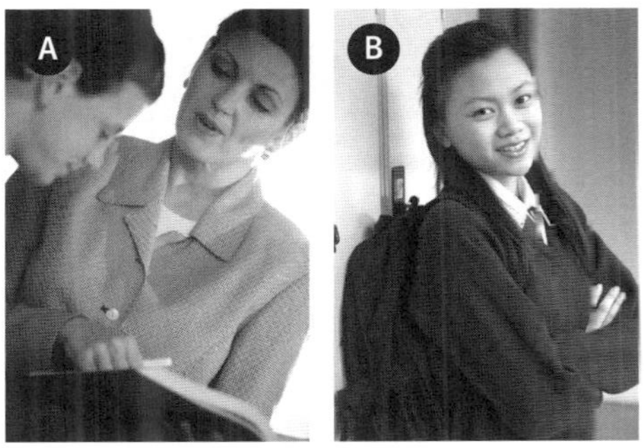

4 A ____
  B ____

Read & listen

6 **09** Read and listen to the text *International workers* on page 24 of the Student's Book.

3B | International train

COLOURS & NATIONALITIES

1 Find seven colour words in the wordsearch.

B	W	B	I	Y	E
L	H	L	E	E	G
A	I	U	R	L	R
C	T	E	E	L	E
K	E	D	D	O	E
O	B	R	O	W	N

2 Choose the correct word to complete the sentences.

1 I'm from *Italy* / *Italian*.
2 He's *France* / *French*.
3 Are you from *Canada* / *Canadian*?
4 Xue Fei is *China* / *Chinese*.
5 Jens and Evi are *Germany* / *German*.
6 This is a *Russian* / *Russia* train.
7 I'm not *Britain* / *British*, I'm Irish.

TO BE (NEGATIVE)

3 Complete the sentences with *'m not, isn't* or *aren't*.

A: Look! Is that a student from your class?

B: He (1) _________ a student. He's the teacher!

A: Are the teachers at your school from the US?

B: No, they (2) __________. They're British.

C: Are you from Spain?

D: No, I (3) __________. I'm from Italy. My wife's Spanish. Her name's Maria.

C: Is she from Madrid?

D: No, she (4) __________. She's from Barcelona.

4 Decide if the sentences are correct or incorrect. Correct the incorrect sentences.

1 He's isn't from the US.
2 She isn't from Italy, she's from Switzerland.
3 They're on a train.
4 I not am at the hotel.
5 My name isn't Chloë, it's Ellie.

TRANSLATION

5 Translate the sentences into your language.

1 He's from the US.

____.

2 I'm not French.

____.

3 The Canadian flag is red and white.

____.

4 They aren't from Brazil.

____.

5 This isn't the train to Madrid.

____.

3c | International school

Days of the week

1 Complete the calendar with the days.

MAY

- **11** Monday
- **12** (1) ____________
- **13** (2) ____________
- **14** Thursday
- **15** (3) ____________
- **16** (4) ____________
- **17** Sunday

To be (questions & short answers)

2 Rearrange the words to make questions or short answers.

1 are you from Where ?

____

2 from Is the US he ?

____

3 they Australian Are ?

____

4 No, not I'm .

____

5 is he Yes, .

____

3 Match the questions 1–5 to the answers a–e.

1	Are you from Germany?	a ☐	Yes, you are.
2	Is she a teacher?	b ☐	No, it isn't.
3	Are they in London?	c [1]	No, I'm not.
4	Is the school open on Saturday?	d ☐	Yes, she is.
5	Am I in this class?	e ☐	Yes, they are.

The classroom

4 Complete the expressions with words from the box.

spell Wednesday English

1

2

3

Dictation

5 **10** Write the sentences that you hear.

1 ______________________________?

2 ______________________________.

3 ______________________________.

4 ______________________________.

5 ______________________________.

Read & listen

6 **11** Read and listen to the text *United Nations International School* on page 28 of the Student's Book.

3 | Test yourself

Vocabulary

1 Complete the table with the words from the box.

actor Brazil China doctor French
Friday German blue Tuesday yellow

JOB	COUNTRY	NATIONALITY	COLOUR	DAY

/5

2 Complete the sentences with the words from the box.

diplomat France French green Wednesday

1 She's from ______.
2 My birthday is on ______.
3 Emma's favourite colour is ______.
4 Is he ______?
5 Her father is a ______.

/5

Grammar

3 Choose the correct word to complete the sentences.

1 She *am* / *are* / *isn't* a doctor.
2 What nationality *am* / *are* / *is* you?
3 I *'m* / *aren't* / *is* Brazilian.
4 What day *am* / *are* / *is* it today?
5 No, they *isn't* / *are* / *aren't*.

/5

4 Write questions using the prompts.

1 Where / you / from

______________________________?

2 she / French

______________________________?

3 What / your / job

______________________________?

4 you / a police officer

______________________________?

5 Yukiko / from Japan

______________________________?

/5

Functional language

5 Complete the sentences with the words and phrases from the box.

don't you do you on do you your job

1 What do ______________?
2 What's ______________?
3 How ______________ pronounce it?
4 Sorry, I ______________ understand.
5 See ______________ Wednesday.

/5

Total: /25

4A Personal photos

Numbers 21–101

1 Tick (✓) the correct word, a or b.

1 30 a) thirty ____
b) twenty ____

2 14 a) forty ____
b) fourteen ____

3 50 a) fifteen ____
b) fifty ____

4 99 a) ninety-nine ____
b) nineteen ____

5 24 a) twenty-five ____
b) twenty-four ____

2 Complete the table with the correct numbers.

61	(1) *sixty-one*
70	(2) ____________
(3) ____________	eighty-six
47	(4) ____________
(5) ____________	fifty-nine
101	(6) ____________

Talking about age

3 Look at the photos and the information. Write questions and answers.

1 15 years / car
How old is the car?
The car is fifteen years old.

2 60 years / computer
________________________?
________________________.

3 18 months / houses
________________________?
________________________.

4 33 years / school
________________________?
________________________.

5 101 years / man
________________________?
________________________.

It, they

4 Replace the underlined words with *he*, *she*, *it* or *they*.

1 The car is fifteen years old. *It*
2 How old are the babies? ________
3 Where are the glasses? ________
4 The woman is 28 years old. ________
5 My doctor is a young man. ________
6 Your wallet is on the table. ________
7 The computers aren't old. ________

Dictation

5 **12** Write the sentences that you hear.

1 ________________________________?
2 ________________________________.
3 ________________________________.
4 ________________________________.
5 ________________________________?

4B Personal web page

Family

1 Complete the sentences with the words from the box.

son	grandparents	husband	daughter
children	~~parents~~		

1 Your mother and father are your *parents.*

2 Your grandfather and grandmother are your ______.

3 They are married. She is his wife and he is her ______.

4 She is my sister. She is my parents' ______.

5 He is my brother. He is my parents' ______.

6 Your son and your daughter are your ______.

2 Choose the correct words to complete the text.

on the left **on the right**

This is a photo of my brother's wedding day. This is my brother and his (1) *wife / husband.* Her name is Laura. On the left are Laura's (2) *children / parents*, Jenny and Graham. There's Laura's (3) *sister / brother*, Sarah and her husband on the left, too. I'm on the right with my brother, Robert. My (4) *mother / father* is there, too. Her name is Virginia. My sister, Diana, is in the photo, too.

Listening

3 **13** Listen and tick (✓) the correct sentence, a or b.

1 a) The women are sisters. ____
b) The women are mother and daughter. ____

2 a) The man's mother is from Italy. ____
b) The man is from Italy. ____

3 a) The woman's son is eighteen months old. ____
b) The woman's son is eighteen years old. ____

Possessive *'s*

4 Look at the pictures and write sentences using the prompts.

John / dog

1 It *is John's dog.*

the President / house

2 It ______________________.

the baby / juice

3 It ______________________.

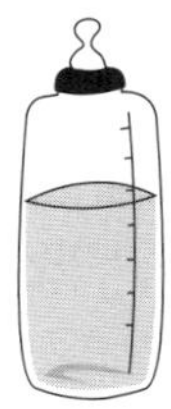

the children / sandwiches

4 They ______________________.

the teacher / book

5 It ______________________.

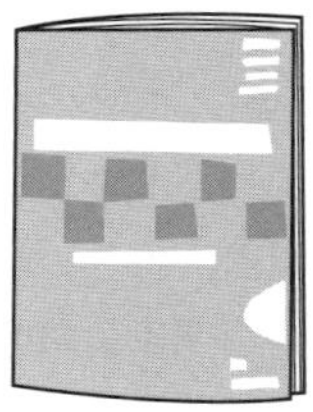

Read & listen

5 **14** Read and listen to the web page *Michael and Jennifer Murphy's family album* on page 34 of the Student's Book.

4c | Personal possessions

Prepositions of place

1 Look at the picture and choose the correct preposition to complete the sentences.

1 The books are *on* / *under* the chair.
2 The computer is *on* / *under* the table.
3 The table is *next to* / *under* the chair.
4 The coffee is *in* / *next to* the computer.
5 The books are *in* / *on* the bag.

2 Write more sentences about the picture in exercise 1 with the prompts.

1 The bag / the chair

The bag is under the chair.

2 The jacket / the chair

______________________________.

3 The ID card / the jacket

______________________________.

4 The keys / the computer

______________________________.

5 The keys / the table

______________________________.

Personal possessions

3 Find seven personal possessions in the wordsearch.

M	K	I	W	W	L	E	E	J	I
O	E	C	J	A	N	Y	T	H	K
B	T	M	A	T	P	O	H	J	K
I	A	P	C	R	E	U	P	O	E
L	C	O	K	P	E	M	G	K	T
E	B	K	E	Y	S	B	L	S	P
P	H	O	T	O	L	R	A	Z	J
H	E	S	H	R	R	E	S	E	E
O	E	I	E	L	A	L	S	A	J
N	A	O	W	A	L	L	E	T	O
E	S	J	U	A	E	A	S	N	E

Translation

4 Translate the sentences into your language.

1 The school is next to my house.

______________________________.

2 Where's my jacket?

______________________________?

3 It's behind you.

______________________________.

4 The taxi is in front of the hotel.

______________________________.

5 The hotel is in Bangkok.

______________________________.

4 | Test yourself

Functional language

1 Rearrange the words to make sentences or questions.

1 you How are old ?

____

2 sixty-five old years He's .

____

3 a It's computer new .

____

4 they are old How ?

____

5 man young a He's .

____

/5

Vocabulary

2 Look at the pictures and complete the sentences.

1 It's *a mobile phone.*

2 It's _______________.

3 It's _______________.

4 It's _______________.

5 It's _______________.

6 It's _______________.

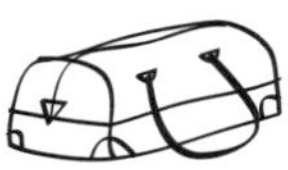

/5

3 Complete the sentences using the family tree.

Helga = Ian
|
John = Camilla
|
Justin   Amy

1 John is Camilla's _______.
2 Justin is Amy's _______.
3 Amy is Justin's _______.
4 Camilla and John are Amy's _______.
5 Ian is Justin's _______.

/5

Grammar

4 Tick (✓) the correct sentence, a or b.

1 a) This is Michael father's. ____
  b) This is Michael's father. ____
2 a) It's my grandparent's house. ____
  b) It's my grandparents' house. ____
3 a) They are sisters. ____
  b) They are sister's. ____
4 a) The telephone is on the table. ____
  b) The telephone is in the table. ____
5 a) The jacket is next of the bag. ____
  b) The jacket is next to the bag. ____

/5

5 Replace the <u>underlined</u> words with the correct pronoun.

1 My house is in Spain. <u>My house</u> is in Madrid. _______
2 Sarah is a teacher. <u>Sarah</u> is from Britain. _______
3 <u>Jenny and Graham</u> are my parents. _______
4 <u>Your glasses</u> are on the table. _______
5 <u>My brother</u> is 40 years old. _______

/5

Total: /25

3 & 4 | Reading

1 Read the profiles 1–4 and match them to the photos A–D.

A ☐

B ☐

C ☐

D ☐

File Edit View Favourites Tools Help Links »

The Jacobson Family

1	2	3	4
Profile:	**Profile:**	**Profile:**	**Profile:**
Last name: Jacobson	Last name: Jacobson	Last name: Jacobson	Last name: Jacobson
First name: Junko	First name: Hannah	First name: Mats	First name: Bjorn
Nationality: Japanese	Nationality: Swedish	Nationality: Swedish	Nationality: Swedish
Age: 33	Age: 12	Age: 6	Age: 45
Job: Teacher	Job: Student	Job: Student	Job: Diplomat

2 Read the text about the Jacobson family. <u>Underline</u> the incorrect information. Then write the correct word above.

The Jacobson Family

Sweden

These are the Jacobsons. Bjorn is from <u>Japan</u>. He's forty-six years old and he's a diplomat. Junko is Bjorn's husband. She isn't Swedish, she's Japanese. She's a student and she's thirty-three years old. Their children are Hannah and Mats. They're teachers. Hannah is eleven years old and Mats is six years old. They're Japanese

READ & LISTEN

3 **15** Listen to Reading 3 & 4 *The Jacobson Family* on the CD. Check your answers to exercise 2.

5A | Working life

Common verbs & nouns (1)

1 Complete the sentences with *live*, *work* or *go*.

1 I *work* in a shop.

2 I _________ with my parents.

3 I _________ in a shop in Mexico City.

4 We _________ to work on foot.

5 They _________ in a factory.

6 We _________ to school by bus.

2 Choose the correct word to complete the sentences.

1 I live *in* / *from* Casablanca.
2 I live *in* / *with* my wife and two sons.
3 We live *in* / *on* a house.
4 I work *for* / *by* a company.
5 My wife works *with* / *in* a shop.
6 We go to work *by* / *on* car.

Present simple (1) (affirmative)

3 Complete the text with the verbs in brackets in the present simple.

Katja (1) *is* (*be*) from Ukraine. She (2) _____ (*live*) with her husband and her grandfather. They (3) _____ (*live*) in Odessa. Katja (4) _____ (*be*) an English teacher. She (5) _____ (*work*) in a school in the city centre. She (6) _____ (*go*) to work on foot. Katja's husband and her grandfather (7) _____ (*work*) in a big factory. The factory (8) _____ (be) next to the city. They (9) _____ (*go*) to work by train.

4 Choose the correct word to complete the sentences.

1 *It* / *They* live in a small town in Italy.
2 *I* / *He* works for a small company.
3 *She* / *You* works in a hotel.
4 *I* / *He* go to work by bus.
5 *They* / *She* goes to school on foot.

Listening

5 **16** Listen and decide if the sentences are true (T) or false (F). Correct the false sentences.

1 He is from London. ______
2 He lives in London. ______
3 He works in a factory. ______
4 His wife works in a school. ______
5 His wife goes to school on foot. ______
6 His wife is from Britain. ______

Read & listen

6 **17** Read and listen to the article *Working life* on page 43 of the Student's Book.

5B | Technology life

Technology

1 Look at the advertisement and complete the sentences.

1 The *computer* is 800 euros.

2 The __________ is 69 euros.

3 The __________ is 329 euros.

4 The __________ is 129 euros.

5 The __________ is 99 euros.

6 The __________ is 30 euros.

Present simple (2) (negative; *and* & *but*)

2 Complete the sentences with information from the table.

	Chris	Janet
have a computer at home	✓	✗
have a computer at work	✓	✗
have a digital camera	✗	✗
write emails	✓	✗
have a game console	✗	✓
have a mobile phone	✓	✓

1 Chris *has* a computer at home.

2 Janet ________ a computer at work.

3 Chris ________ a computer at work.

4 Chris and Janet ________ a digital camera.

5 Janet ________ emails.

6 Chris ________ a game console.

7 Janet and Chris ________ a mobile phone.

3 Complete the sentences so they are true for you.

1 I ________ (*have*) a computer at home.

2 I ________ (*have*) a mobile phone.

3 I ________ (*have*) my mobile phone in class.

4 I ________ (*use*) the internet at work/school.

4 Choose the correct word to complete the sentences.

1 He has a computer *and* / *but* she has a computer.
2 He has a computer, *and* / *but* he doesn't use it.
3 She has a computer *and* / *but* she uses it.
4 She uses the internet *and* / *but* she writes emails.
5 He has a mobile phone, *and* / *but* he doesn't have a work telephone.

Dictation

5 **18** Write the email or website addresses that you hear.

1 ________________________________

2 ________________________________

3 ________________________________

4 ________________________________

5 ________________________________

5c | Hard life?

Adjectives (1)

1 Look at the pictures and complete the sentences with an adjective.

1 It's a b*ad* day.

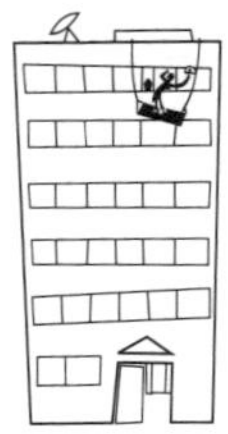

2 She has a d________ job.

3 He has an e________ job.

4 It's a g________ day.

5 This is an i________ class.

2 Decide if the sentences are correct or incorrect. Correct the incorrect sentences.

1 Today I start a job new.

2 I work in a big city.

3 It isn't a job boring.

4 It isn't a difficult job.

5 It's interesting.

6 I work for a company big.

Present simple (3) (questions & short answers)

3 Choose the correct word to complete the questions.

1 *Do / Does* your father have a difficult job?
2 *Do / Does* she work in a school?
3 *Do / Does* he work alone?
4 *Do / Does* your parents work Monday to Friday?
5 *Do / Does* you go to work by car?

4 Match the questions 1–5 from exercise 3 to the answers a–e.

☐ a No, I don't. I go to work by train.

☐ b No, he doesn't. He works in an office with other people.

☐ c Yes, she does. Her school is next to my house.

☐ d No, he doesn't. It's an easy job.

☐ e No, they don't. They don't work on Monday.

Translation

5 Translate the sentences into your language.

1 It's a boring job.

____.

2 Do you work in an office?

____?

3 Does he live here?

____?

4 He works in London, but he doesn't live there.

____.

5 | Test yourself

Vocabulary

1 Complete the text with the words from the box.

flat   bus   factory   parents   foot

Valerie and Janet are sisters. They work in a (1) __________ in Manchester. Valerie lives in a (2) __________. She lives next to the factory and she goes to work on (3) __________. Janet lives with her (4) __________. She goes to work by (5) __________.

/5

2 Match the words 1–5 to the opposites a–e.

1 difficult   ☐ a new
2 good   ☐ b white
3 interesting   ☐ c boring
4 old   ☐ d easy
5 black   ☐ e bad

/5

Grammar

3 Write sentences or questions in the present simple using the prompts.

1 He / not live / in Germany

__________________________.

2 He / live / in Belgium

__________________________.

3 she / work / in Beijing

__________________________?

4 they / go / to school / by bus

__________________________?

5 He / have / computer / but / not use it

__________________________.

/5

4 Write short answers.

1 Do they work for the US government? ☑ *Yes, they do.*
2 Do they work in Washington? ☑ __________.
3 Does she live in Washington? ☒ __________.
4 Do they go to work by bus? ☒ __________.
5 Does he use a computer at work? ☑ __________.
6 Do they have a difficult job? ☑ __________.

/5

Functional language

5 Tick (✓) the correct address, a or b.

1 fotx.col
  a) fotx dot col ____
  b) fotx at col ____
2 jamie@email.col
  a) jamie at email dot col ____
  b) jamie slash email dot col ____
3 english.col/information
  a) english dot col at information ____
  b) english dot col slash information ____
4 teacher@english.co.ur
  a) teacher at english dot co dot ur ____
  b) teacher dot english dot co dot ur ____
5 adrian.tennant@work.col
  a) adrian dot tennant at work dot col ____
  b) adrian at tennant at work dot col ____

/5

Total: /25

6A | Daytime

Common verbs & nouns (2)

1 Complete the texts with the verbs from the box.

drink	eat (x2)	go (x2)	read (x2)	wake up (x2)

My name is Mandy Stewart and I'm a morning person. I (1) ______ at six o'clock. I (2) _____ a coffee and (3) ______ the newspaper. I (4) ______ a big breakfast and then I (5) _____ to work.

I'm Wendy Stewart, Mandy's sister. I'm not a morning person. I like to (6) ______ a book in bed and I (7) ______ to bed late. I often (8) ______ late. In the morning I never (9) ______ breakfast, I sometimes don't have time for coffee. I'm always late – for class, for the bus, for work ...

2 Read the texts in exercise 1 again and write *M* (for Mandy) or *W* (for Wendy) next to the correct pictures.

Adverbs of frequency

3 Rearrange the words to make sentences.

1 drink I a cup of coffee usually .

____

2 often They tired are .

____

3 breakfast hardly ever I eat .

____

4 to work He walks sometimes .

____

Telling the time (1)

4 Look at the clocks and choose the correct time from the times in the box.

It's eleven o'clock.	It's four thirty.
It's seven forty am.	It's two forty-five.
It's one twenty pm.	~~It's seven fifteen.~~

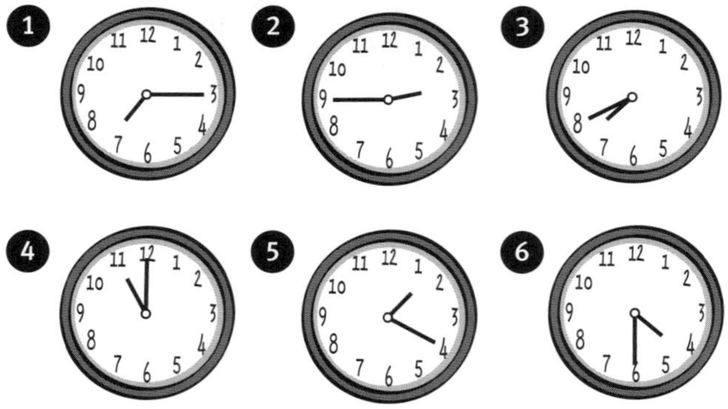

1 *It's seven fifteen.*
2 ______________.
3 ______________.
4 ______________.
5 ______________.
6 ______________.

Translation

5 Translate the sentences into your language.

1 I always eat breakfast.

______________________________.

2 I usually get up at seven o'clock.

______________________________.

3 What time is it?

______________________________?

4 It's 8pm.

______________________________.

Read & listen

6 **19** Read and listen to the article *Morning people and night people* on page 50 of the Student's Book.

6B | Free time

Common verbs & nouns (3); free time activities

1 Complete the sentences with *play*, *read* or *learn* and the words from the box.

golf   English   ~~football~~   to dance   a book

1 Come and *play football*.

2 It's good to ________________.

3 They ________________ every Saturday.

4 We ________________ with *Straightforward*.

5 Come and ________________ salsa every Wednesday evening.

Present simple (4) (*wh*- questions)

2 Choose the correct word to complete the questions.

1 *When / What / Where* do you do in your free time?
2 *Who / What / Where* do you play it?
3 *When / Who / What* does it start?
4 *When / Who / How* do you play with?
5 *What / When / How* much does it cost?

3 Match the questions 1–5 from exercise 2 to the answers a–e.

☐ a At seven o'clock every Wednesday and Saturday.
☐ b Three euros.
☐ c At the sports centre.
☐ d I play basketball.
☐ e With my friends.

Telling the time (2)

4 Tick (✓) the correct sentences. Correct the incorrect sentences.

1 It's ten to eight. ✓

2 It's a quarter to four. ____

3 It's twenty to ten. ____

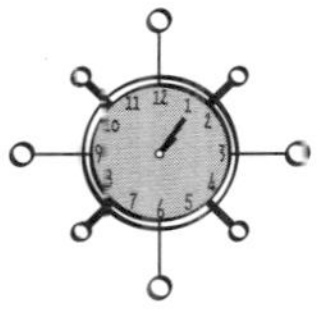

4 It's five past one. ____

5 It's ten to three. ____

Dictation

5 **20** Write the sentences that you hear.

1 ________________________________.
2 ________________________________?
3 ________________________________?
4 ________________________________?
5 ________________________________.

Read & listen

6 **21** Read and listen to the community centre noticeboard notices on page 52 of the Student's Book.

6c | Meal time

Food (2) & meals

1 Complete the crossword.

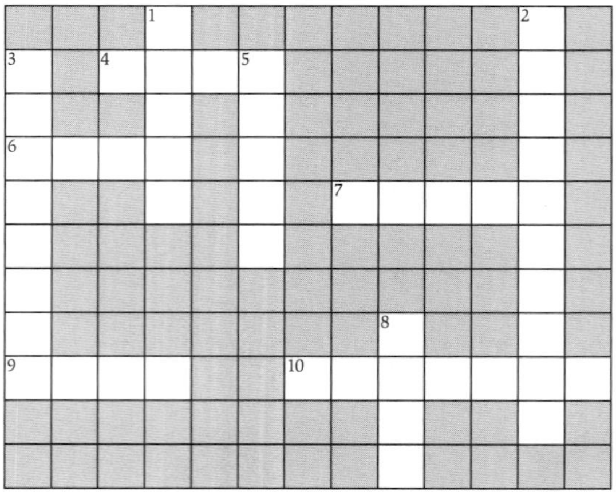

Across

4 

6 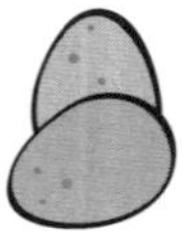

7 

9 

10 

Down

1 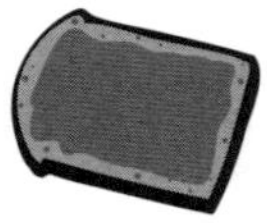

2 

3 

5 

8 

Present simple + *how often* + time expressions

2 Look at the pictures and write sentences using the prompts.

1 Mandy / early every day

Mandy wakes up early every day.

2 Alex / three times a day

______________________________.

3 Simone / her mother / once a week

______________________________.

4 I / once a month

______________________________.

3 Rearrange the words to make questions.

1 do eat often you How fish ?

____

2 breakfast you often do How have ?

____

3 often tea does drink she How ?

____

4 have often does How he lunch at work ?

____

5 do a meal often have at a restaurant How they ?

____

Listening

4 **22** Listen and choose the correct word or phrase to complete the sentences.

1 Frances usually wakes up at half past *five / six*.
2 She drinks *coffee / orange juice* and eats toast for breakfast.
3 She eats *meat / fish* twice a week.
4 She eats with her family once *a week / a month*.
5 She goes to bed after twelve o'clock *twice a week / every day*.

6 | Test yourself

Vocabulary

1 Match the verbs 1–6 to the words a–f.

1	eat	☐	a	a book
2	learn	☐	b	work
3	drink	[1]	c	lunch
4	go to	☐	d	tea
5	read	☐	e	tennis
6	play	☐	f	to dance

[/5]

2 Rearrange the letters to make food words. Match the words 1–5 to the pictures A–E.

1 laasd ____________ 4 hiccenk ____________
2 trufi ____________ 5 stoat ____________
3 gesetvebal ____________

A ☐

B ☐
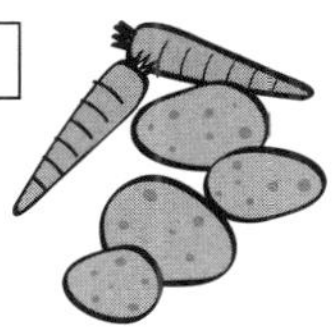

C ☐
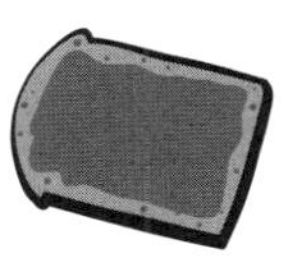

D ☐

E ☐

[/5]

Functional language

3 Complete the sentences.

1 2.00 It's ____________ o' ____________.
2 5.30 It's ____________ ____________ five.
3 6.50 It's ten ____________ ____________.
4 6.15 It's a ____________ ____________ six.
5 12.05 It's five ____________ ____________.

[/5]

Grammar

4 Rewrite the sentences with the words in brackets.

1 I drink a cup of coffee in the morning. (*always*)
____
2 He is tired in the evening. (*often*)
____
3 They go to work at nine o'clock. (*usually*)
____
4 Pete and Sally play tennis on Saturday afternoon. (*sometimes*)
____
5 I am late for class. (*never*)
____

[/5]

5 Match the questions 1–5 to the answers a–e.

1 How much does it cost?
2 How often do you go?
3 What do you do in your free time?
4 When is the class?
5 Where do you go to learn to dance salsa?

☐ a I learn to dance salsa with my friends.
☐ b The community centre.
☐ c Nothing. It's free.
☐ d Twice a week.
☐ e It's on Monday and Friday at seven o'clock in the evening.

[/5]

Total: [/25]

5 & 6 | Reading

The two Charlie Jacksons

My name is Charlie Jackson and I'm 21 years old. I'm from Australia. I live in Sydney. I live with my family. I work in a community centre. I work Monday to Friday and I always go to work by bus. I usually play tennis on Saturday.

Hi! I'm Charlie Jackson. I'm 26 years old and I live in Prague, but I'm not from the Czech Republic. I'm British. I live with two friends. I go to a university here. I usually go to university on foot. Every Saturday I meet my friends for coffee.

Note: In English, Charlie is usually a man's name (Charles) but can sometimes be a woman's name (Charlotte).

1 Read the article and tick (✓) the information it contains.

1 work ____
2 free time ____
3 technology ____
4 university ____
5 time ____

2 Read the article again and complete the sentences with *He* or *She*.

1 ______ goes to work by bus.
2 ______ goes to university on foot.
3 ______ doesn't go to university.
4 ______ works in a community centre.
5 ______ doesn't work.
6 ______ doesn't work on Saturday.
7 ______ doesn't live in Australia.

READ & LISTEN

3 **23** Listen to Reading 5 & 6 *The two Charlie Jacksons* on the CD and read the article again.

7A | City break

Places in a city (1)

1 Complete the travel brochure with the words from the box.

River	Bridge	taxi	Station

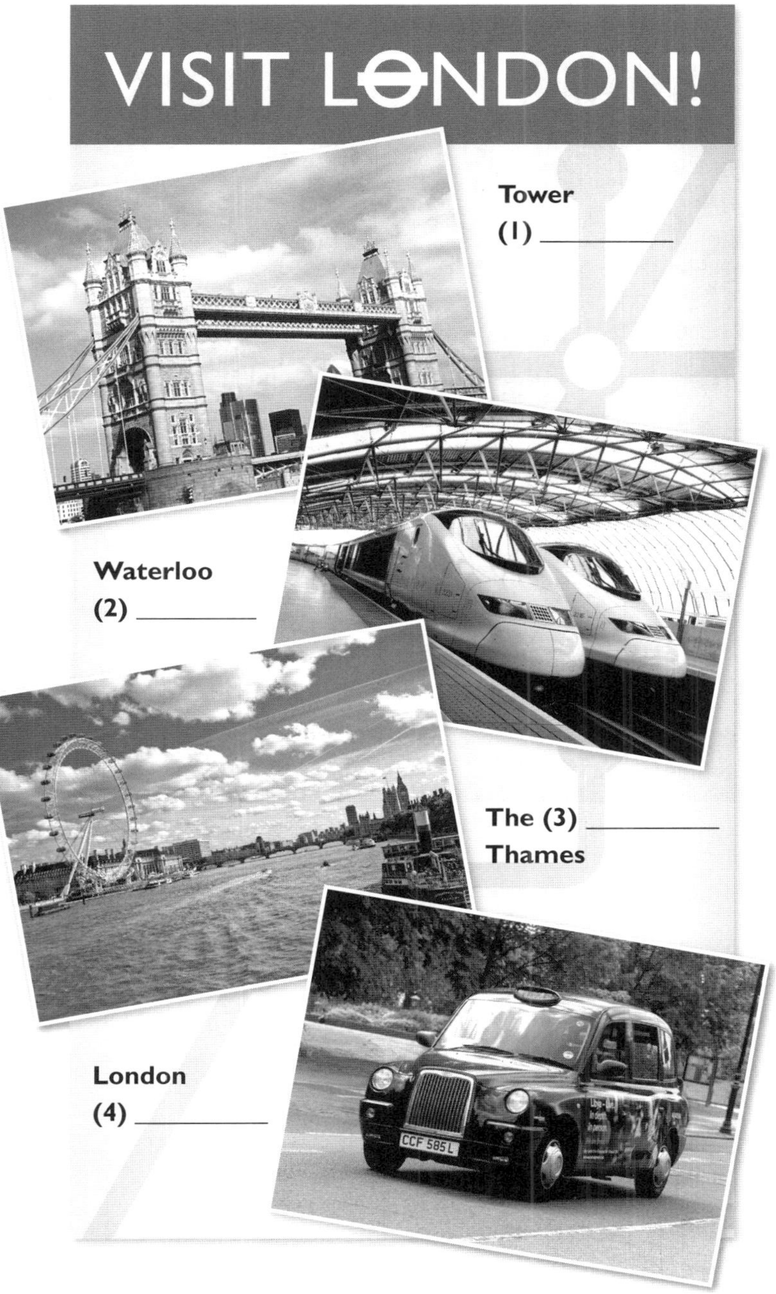

There is/there are (1)

2 Complete the sentences with *is* or *are*.

1 There ______ an airport in the city.
2 There ______ buses to the airport every ten minutes.
3 There ______ a shop in the museum.
4 There ______ people in the shop.
5 There ______ a beach 20 kilometres from here.
6 There ______ a train to the beach.

3 Look at the picture and write sentences using *There is* or *There are*.

1 ______________________________.
2 ______________________________.
3 ______________________________.
4 ______________________________.

Translation

4 Translate the sentences into your language.

1 There are beaches next to the city.

______________________________.

2 Is there a hospital near here?

______________________________?

3 There's a park in front of my house.

______________________________.

4 There are two hotels in the city centre.

______________________________.

Read & listen

5 **24** Read and listen to the magazine page *Take a break in the world's top cities* on page 61 of the Student's Book.

7B | City life

ADJECTIVES (2); PLACES IN A CITY (2)

1 Complete the sentences with the adjectives from the box.

small	unfriendly	expensive	beautiful

1 He's an __________ man.

2 That's an __________ car.

3 The flower is very __________.

4 The sandwiches are very __________.

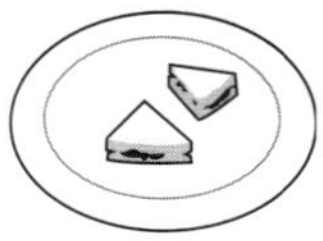

2 Rearrange the letters to make words for places in a city.

1 knab ______________
2 spothail ______________
3 perkartemus ______________
4 aktmre ______________
5 posh ______________

THERE IS/THERE ARE (2) (QUESTIONS & NEGATIVE)

3 Write questions using the prompts.

1 / shops
Are there any shops?

2 / parks
______________________________?

3 / hospital
______________________________?

4 / restaurants
______________________________?

5 / hotels
______________________________?

6 / train station
______________________________?

4 Read the information about Hampstead, London. Write answers to the questions from exercise 3.

1 ______________________________.
2 ______________________________.
3 ______________________________.
4 ______________________________.
5 ______________________________.
6 ______________________________.

LISTENING

5 **25** Listen and decide if the sentences are true (T) or false (F). Correct the false sentences.

1 Roberta is new in the building. ___
2 There isn't a supermarket in the neighbourhood. ___
3 Roberta doesn't have a map. ___
4 There are good shops in the neighbourhood. ___

7c | City tour

Listening

1 **26** Listen and decide if the sentences are true (T) or false (F). Correct the false sentences.

1 The woman wants to go to the cathedral. ___
2 The man can't understand. ___
3 The man speaks English. ___
4 The woman can speak Spanish. ___

Travel words

2 Complete the crossword.

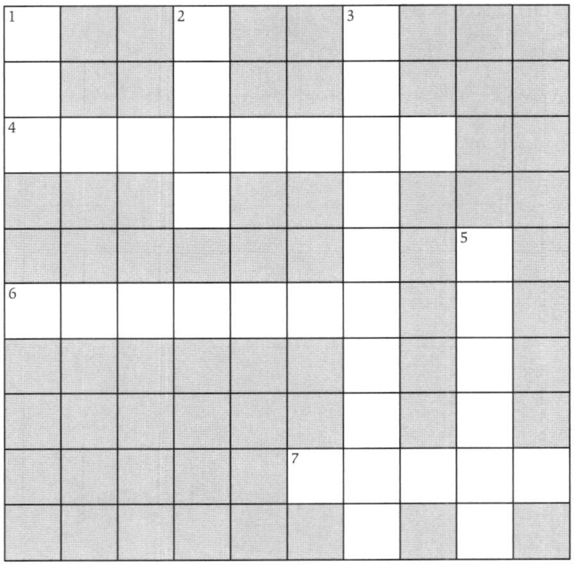

Across

4 

6 

7 

Down

1 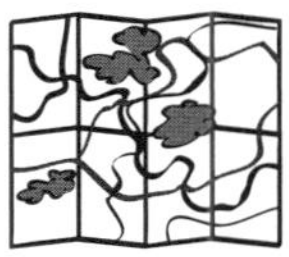

2 

3 

5 

3 Complete the sentences with the words from exercise 2.

1 **A**: Do you have a (1) _________ of the city centre?
B: Yes, we do. Here you are.

2 **C**: How do you say 'Excuse me?' in Chinese?
D: Look in your Chinese/English (2) _________.

3 **E**: Can I have a return (3) _________ to Oxford, please?
F: Of course. Here you are.

4 **G**: Hello. Welcome to the United States. Can I see your (4) _________?
H: Yes, here you are.
G: Thank you. You're from Italy?
H: Yes, that's right.

Survival English

4 Correct one mistake in each sentence or question.

1 I no speak English.
2 You speak Spanish?
3 I no understand.
4 You repeat, please?
5 I sorry.

Dictation

5 **27** Write the sentences that you hear.

1 ______________________________.
2 ______________________________.
3 ______________________________.

7 | Test yourself

FUNCTIONAL LANGUAGE

1 Rearrange the words to make sentences or questions.

1 I understand don't .

____

2 Chinese you Do speak ?

____

3 you repeat, please Can ?

____

4 speak a only little I English .

____

5 speak don't English I .

____

/5

VOCABULARY

2 Underline the adjectives in the text and match them to the opposites 2–5.

1 This is my flat. I live here with two friends. It's not very big and it's ugly. It's not a good flat, but it's cheap.

2 ____________ beautiful

3 ____________ expensive

4 ____________ bad

5 ____________ small

/5

GRAMMAR

3 Make sentences about Hotel Club ***, using *There is* or *There are*.

HOTEL CLUB ***

80 rooms
A café
Wifi in every room
Three meeting rooms
Two restaurants
Indoor swimming pool

1 *There are 80 rooms.*

2 ______________________________.

3 ______________________________.

4 ______________________________.

5 ______________________________.

6 ______________________________.

/10

4 Choose the correct words to complete the dialogue.

A: (1) *Is / Are* there a bank near here?
B: No, there (2) *isn't / is*. There (3) *is / are* banks in the city centre.
A: Do you have a map?
B: Yes, here you are.
A: Thank you. (4) *Is / Are* there a bus or train to the city centre?
B: Yes, there (5) *is / are* buses every ten minutes.
A: Thank you.
B: You're welcome.

/5

Total: /25

8A | Film sequels

WAS/WERE

1 Complete the texts with *was* or *were*.

The first *Pirates of the Caribbean* film (1) ______ made in 2003. The actors (2) ______ Johnny Depp, Orlando Bloom and Keira Knightley. In 2006 there (3) ______ a sequel – *Pirates of the Caribbean: Dead Man's Chest*. All three original actors (4) ______ in the sequel. There are now four *Pirates of the Caribbean* films.

Psycho is a very famous film by Alfred Hitchcock. It (5) ________ very popular when it (6) ________ in the cinemas in 1960. The actors (7) ________ Anthony Perkins and Janet Leigh. The remake (8) ________ in 1998. The actors Vince Vaughn and Anne Heche (9) ________ in the remake.

2 Tick (✓) the correct sentence a or b.

1 a) You was at home last night. ____
  b) You were at home last night ____

2 a) I was with my girlfriend. ____
  b) I were with my girlfriend. ____

3 a) We was at the cinema. ____
  b) We were at the cinema. ____

4 a) The film was very good. ____
  b) The film were very good. ____

5 a) It was a popular film. ____
  b) It were a popular film. ____

6 a) The seats was cheap. ____
  b) The seats were cheap. ____

YEARS

3 Write the years in numbers.

1 two thousand and eight *2008*
2 nineteen ninety ____________
3 nineteen seventy-four ____________
4 two thousand and twelve ____________
5 two thousand ____________
6 nineteen forty-four ____________
7 nineteen twelve ____________

DICTATION

4 **28** Write the sentences that you hear.

1 ____.
2 ____.
3 ____.
4 ____.

READ & LISTEN

5 **29** Read and listen to the article *Do it again* on page 68 of the Student's Book.

8B | Film script

Was/were (questions, negative & time expressions)

1 Complete the sentences with *was*, *were*, *wasn't* or *weren't*.

1 Mr Magnus *wasn't* (–) at home yesterday.
2 Mr Magnus *was* (+) at the factory.
3 The fire __________ (+) last night.
4 Mr Magnus and his wife __________ (+) divorced.
5 His wife's name __________ (+) Janet.
6 Peter Gordon __________ (–) married.
7 Peter Gordon __________ (+) Janet's boyfriend.
8 The two men __________ (–) friends.

2 Write questions using the prompts.

1 he / English
Was he English?
2 he / a real person
____?
3 Where / he from
____?
4 Who / his friend
____?
5 What / his friend's job
____?
6 his house and offices / in London
____?

3 Complete the timeline with the time expressions from the box.

yesterday morning	last night	
last week	last year	last month

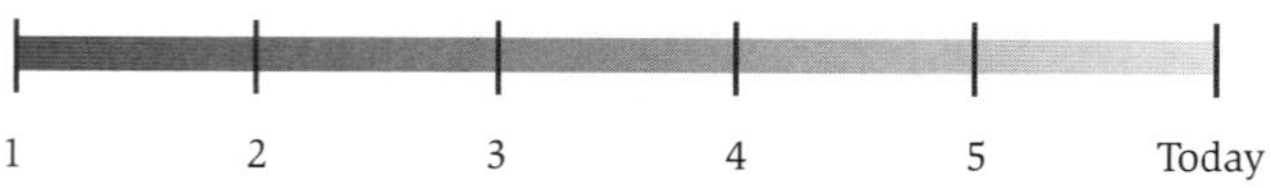

(1) ____________________ (4) ____________________
(2) ____________________ (5) ____________________
(3) ____________________

4 Read the text about Sherlock Holmes and Watson. Write short answers to the questions in exercise 2.

Sherlock Holmes was a famous English detective. He wasn't a real person. He was a character in the books by Sir Arthur Conan Doyle. Sherlock Holmes was from London. Sherlock Holmes was friends with a man called Watson. Watson was a doctor. Sherlock Holmes' house and offices were at 221b Baker Street. It is there today, and many tourists in London visit it every day.

1 Was he English?
Yes, he was.
2 ____.
3 ____.
4 ____.
5 ____.
6 ____.

Listening

5 **30** Listen and choose the correct word or phrase to complete the sentences.

1 Janet Smith is Mr Magnus' *ex-wife* / *wife*.
2 They were married for *five years* / *ten years*.
3 Janet Smith and Peter Gordon were *married* / *friends*.
4 Janet *wasn't in love* / *was in love* with Peter.
5 Last night Janet was *with Peter* / *at the factory*.

8c | Film reviews

Adjectives of opinion & giving an opinion

1 Write questions using the prompts.

1 like / the beach
Do you like the beach?
2 think / Italian food
What do you think of Italian food?
3 think / comedy films
____________________?
4 like / watching football
____________________?
5 think / Chinese food
____________________?
6 like / planes
____________________?

2 Write answers to the questions in exercise 1 so they are true for you.

1 *I don't like the beach.*
2 *I think Italian food is great.*
3 ____________________.
4 ____________________.
5 ____________________.
6 ____________________.

Subject & object pronouns

3 Complete the table with the correct pronouns.

subject	object
I	(1) ______
(2) ______	you
he	(3) ______
(4) ______	her
it	(5) ______
(6) ______	us
they	(7) ______

4 Replace the underlined words with pronouns.

1 His name is Pablo. <u>His name</u> is a Spanish name. ______
2 He often travels on aeroplanes, but he doesn't like <u>aeroplanes</u>. ______
3 <u>Antonio Banderas and Penélope Cruz</u> are from Spain. ______
4 My wife's parents live with <u>my wife and me</u>. ______
5 That man is my doctor. I don't like <u>that man</u>. ______

Translation

5 Translate the sentences into your language.

1 What do you think of the film?
____________________?
2 I like it. It's great.
____________________.
3 I love you. Do you love me?
____________________?
4 He doesn't like them.
____________________.
5 The food is awful.
____________________.

8 | Test yourself

FUNCTIONAL LANGUAGE

1 What do they think? Tick (✓) the correct symbol, a, b or c.

1 'The film was OK.'
a) ☺ ____ b) 😐 ____ c) ☹ ____

2 'I love it.'
a) ☺ ____ b) 😐 ____ c) ☹ ____

3 'We think he's great.'
a) ☺ ____ b) 😐 ____ c) ☹ ____

4 'I don't like it.'
a) ☺ ____ b) 😐 ____ c) ☹ ____

5 'I hate it.'
a) ☺ ____ b) 😐 ____ c) ☹ ____

/5

VOCABULARY

2 Tick (✓) the correct number, a or b.

1 2010
a) two hundred and ten ____
b) two thousand and ten ____

2 1918
a) nineteen eighty ____
b) nineteen eighteen ____

3 1980
a) nineteen eighty ____
b) nineteen eighteen ____

4 2000
a) two thousand ____
b) two thousands ____

5 1998
a) nineteen ninety-eighteen ____
b) nineteen ninety-eight ____

/5

GRAMMAR

3 Complete the text with the correct form of the verb *to be* in the past simple.

My favourite TV show (1) *was* (+) *Miami Vice*. It (2) ______ (+) a US police television show in the 1980s. The actors in *Miami Vice* (3) ______ (+) Don Johnson and Philip Michael Thomas. They (4) ______ (–) very good actors. The show (5) ______ (+) in Miami. Colin Farrell and Jamie Foxx (6) ______ (+) in the 2006 remake.

/5

4 Rearrange the words to make sentences or questions.

1 last work night I at was .
____

2 yesterday you were Where ?
____

3 good It film a wasn't .
____

4 that Who man was ?
____

5 France They from weren't .
____

/5

5 Choose the correct word to complete the dialogues.

1 **A:** What do you think of Coldplay?
B: I don't like *they / them* very much.

2 **C:** Where were you last night?
D: I was with Miriam. *She / Her* is my fiancée.

3 **E:** Do you like *him / he*?
F: No, I don't.

4 **G:** This is John. I work with *he / him*.
H: Nice to meet you.

5 **I:** What do you think of Jane?
J: I like her, but she doesn't like *I / me*.

/5

Total: /25

7 & 8 | Reading

1 Read the web page. Which building is the hotel, A, B, C or D?

File Edit View Favourites Tools Help Links

Home | About | **Hotels** | Activities | Location

Highcroft Park

Location • Prices • Rooms • Contact us • **Address**

Highcroft Park Hotel, 99B Market Street,
Highcroft Springs

The Highcroft Park Hotel is near the beautiful Highcroft Park. It's on Market Street, next to the Royal Bank. In front of the hotel is the famous farmers' market, more than 100 years old.

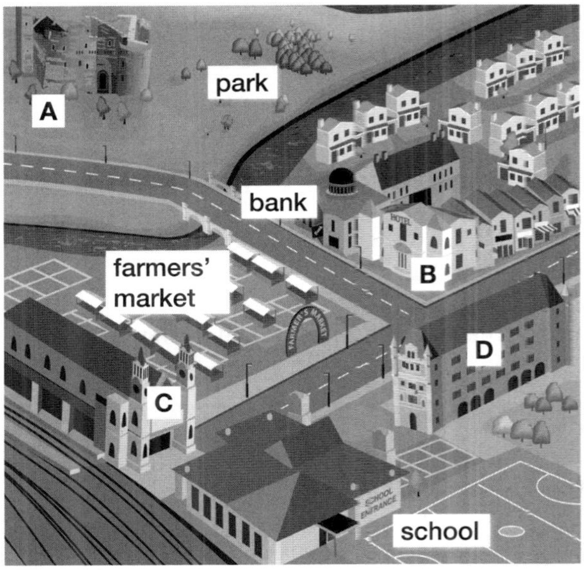

Special weekend break
€60 per person/night
Click here for details.

Highcroft Springs - A *good* place to visit, a *great* place to live

2 Now read about the places on the map and label them.

The train station ____

The train station is on Station Street. It isn't near the park. It's behind the farmers' market and in front of the school.

The city museum ____

The city museum is near the station. It's next to the school on Station Street.

Highcroft Castle ____

The castle is in Highcroft Park near the river. It is near the bridge on Market Street.

Read & listen

3 **31** Listen to Reading 7 & 8 *Highcroft Park* on the CD and read the web page again.

9A | Holiday

Big numbers

1 Complete the table with the correct numbers.

600	(1) ________
(2) ________	one thousand nine hundred
4,000	(3) ________
(4) ________	two hundred thousand
850,000	(5) ________
(6) ________	two million
1,000,000,000	(7) ________

Past simple irregular verbs (affirmative)

2 Complete the text with the past simple of the verbs from the box.

eat go drink see have

Last year I (1) _______ to India on holiday. It was fantastic. I went to New Delhi and Agra. I (2) ________ the famous Taj Mahal. I (3) ________ good Indian food and (4) ________ chai, an Indian tea. I (5) ________ a great time.

3 Write answers to the questions using the prompts.

1 Where did you go?
We / Greece ____________________.

2 What did you see?
We / Pantheon ____________________.

3 What did you eat?
We / moussaka ____________________.

4 What did you drink?
We / orange juice ____________________.

Listening

4 **32** Listen and match the people 1–4 to the places a–d.

1 Bob went to	☐	a the US.
2 Sandie went to	☐	b Spain.
3 Richard went to	☐	c India.
4 Holly went to	☐	d Greece.

Translation

5 Translate the sentences into your language.

1 Last year we went to London.
____________________.

2 I ate British food yesterday.
____________________.

3 The population of London is seven million.
____________________.

4 He saw his friends last night.
____________________.

5 I had a good time.
____________________.

Read & listen

6 **33** Read and listen to the email *Last day of our Indian holiday* on page 78 of the Student's Book.

9B | Last days

Music words

1 Complete the sentences with the words from the box.

concert	crowd	group	songs

1 My mother's favourite ________ were the Beatles.

2 She saw a Beatles ________ in 1964. It was amazing.

3 There were about 500 people in the ________.

4 They played lots of their famous ________, like *A Hard Day's Night* and *She Loves You*.

Past simple regular verbs (affirmative & negative)

2 Make the sentences negative.

1 I listened to the radio last night.
I didn't listen to the radio last night.

2 I went to a concert on Saturday.
____.

3 The Rolling Stones played a concert on the rooftop.
____.

4 The class started at ten o'clock.
____.

5 I wanted to see you yesterday.
____.

6 They arrived late for work last week.
____.

3 Choose the correct word to complete the sentences.

1 The Beatles *play* / *played* their last concert in 1969.
2 They didn't *play* / *played* together again.
3 The concert *start* / *started* at eight o'clock.
4 It didn't *end* / *ended* until after twelve o'clock.
5 I didn't *watch* / *watched* the concert.

Listening

4 **34** Listen and decide if the sentences are true (T) or false (F). Correct the false sentences.

1 The girl was sixteen years old in 1969. ____
2 The girl listened to the Beatles in 1969. ____
3 The man watched Woodstock on TV. ____
4 The man went to Woodstock with his friends. ____
5 The woman's parents had a television in 1969. ____
6 The woman's parents watched the Apollo landing. ____

Read & listen

5 **35** Read and listen to the text about the Beatles' last concert on page 80 of the Student's Book.

9c | Independence day

Months

1 Rearrange the letters to make months. Remember to use capital letters where necessary.

1 lipr**a** ____________
2 runa**j**ay ____________
3 brmove**ne** ____________
4 ly**j**u ____________
5 char**m** ____________
6 b**o**otcre ____________

2 Complete the calendar with the months in exercise 1 in the correct order.

The date

3 Write the ordinal numbers.

1 1st *first*
2 2nd ____________
3 3rd ____________
4 6th ____________
5 9th ____________
6 11th ____________
7 15th ____________
8 21st ____________

Prepositions of time (*in*, *on*, *at*)

4 Choose the correct preposition to complete the sentences.

1 My birthday is *at / in / on* July 27th.
2 Sam was born *at / in / on* 1973.
3 The party starts *at / in / on* nine o'clock.
4 Australia Day is *at / in / on* January every year.
5 Jack always plays football *at / in / on* Saturday.

Dictation

5 **36** Write the sentences that you hear.

1 ____.
2 ____?
3 ____.
4 ____.
5 ____.

9 | Test yourself

Vocabulary

1 Complete the big numbers.

400 four (1) ____________

1,000,000 one (2) ____________

2,500 two (3) ____________ five hundred

400,000 four (4) ____________ (5) ____________

/5

2 Complete the sentences with the words from the box.

February April July September December

1 The ninth month of the year is ____________.

2 There are usually twenty-eight days in ____________.

3 The twelfth month of the year is ____________.

4 The seventh month of the year is ____________.

5 The fourth month of the year is ____________.

/5

Functional language

3 Write the dates.

1 4/7 *fourth of July*

2 1/5 ____________

3 6/11 ____________

4 3/1 ____________

5 21/6 ____________

6 12/8 ____________

/5

Grammar

4 Complete the text with the past simple of the verbs in brackets.

Last year I (1) ____________ (*go*) to New York in July. On 4th July there was a big party to celebrate Independence Day. I (2) ____________ (*not see*) the parades because my friends (3) ____________ (*have*) a barbecue. I (4) ____________ (*eat*) hamburgers but I (5) ____________ (*not drink*) beer. It was a good day.

/5

5 Correct one mistake in each sentence.

1 They didn't had a good time.

2 His birthday is on March.

3 Last year I go on holiday to London.

4 The class starts on six o'clock.

5 I ate pizza and drinked juice.

/5

Total: /25

10A | Good weekend!

Weekend activities

1 Look at the pictures and make sentences using the prompts and the phrases from the box.

~~do the shopping~~ have a big breakfast clean the car make dinner go dancing

1 I / usually / on Saturday
I usually do the shopping on Saturday.

2 I / usually / on Friday evening

______________________________.

3 They / often / at the weekend

______________________________.

4 He / always / on Sunday

______________________________.

5 They / sometimes / at the weekend

______________________________.

Past simple questions (1)

2 Write questions in the past simple using the prompts.

1 you / clean the car
Did you clean the car?

2 you / watch TV

______________________________?

3 you / go out

______________________________?

4 she / see a film

______________________________?

5 he / go to London

______________________________?

6 they / go shopping

______________________________?

3 Put the word *did* in the correct place in the questions.

1 What *did* you do yesterday?

2 You see Marco last night?

3 She phone you this morning?

4 What time he leave?

5 When you start learning English?

6 They go on holiday?

Listening

4 **37** Listen to the three dialogues. Match the dialogues 1–3 to the pictures A–D. There's one extra picture.

A ☐

B ☐

C ☐

D ☐

10B Good question!

Past simple questions (2)

1 Rearrange the words to make questions.

1 the World Cup Italy When did win ?

____

2 write *Romeo and Juliet* Did Shakespeare ?

____

3 concert the Beatles' When last was ?

____

4 India get When its independence from Britain did ?

____

2 Match the questions 1–4 in exercise 1 to the answers a–d.

☐ a In 2006. ☐ c In 1947.

☐ b In January 1969. ☐ d Yes, he did.

3 Write short answers to the questions.

1 Were you at the quiz? (✓)

Yes, I was.

2 Did you know the answers? (✗)

No, I didn't.

3 Did you win a prize? (✗)

______________________________.

4 Were you with your friends? (✓)

______________________________.

5 Did they enjoy it? (✓)

______________________________.

6 Was it your first quiz? (✗)

______________________________.

Guessing

4 Complete the dialogue with the words from the box.

Maybe sure think

A: What's the answer?

B: I (1) __________ it's Britain.

C: I don't know. (2) __________ it's Brazil.

B: No, it's Britain.

A: Are you (3) __________?

Translation

5 Translate the sentences into your language.

1 Did you go out last night?

______________________________?

2 I'm sure it's 1971.

______________________________.

3 When did the Beatles end?

______________________________?

4 What's the answer?

______________________________?

5 Maybe it's London.

______________________________.

Read & listen

6 **38** Read and listen to the text *Quiz night* on page 88 of the Student's Book.

10c | Good deal

In a shop

1 Complete the sentences with the words and phrases from the box.

just looking	How much	help you
credit card	changing rooms	€180

Money & prices

2 Match the symbols 1–5 to the words a–e.

1 £ ☐ a cents
2 $ ☐ b dollars
3 p ☐ c euros
4 c ☐ d pence
5 € ☐ e pounds

3 Write the prices in words.

1 $1.99 *one dollar and ninety-nine cents*
2 $6.49 ________
3 £18.10 ________
4 €1.35 ________
5 $200 ________
6 90p ________

Clothes labels

4 Rearrange the letters to make words.

1 **lsmal** ________
2 **ingriloa** ________
3 **ragle** ________
4 **dimume** ________

Dictation

5 **39** Write the sentences that you hear.

1 ________?
2 ________?
3 ________.
4 ________?
5 ________.

Read & listen

6 **40** Read and listen to the article *Night markets – the place for a good deal* on page 90 of the Student's Book.

10 Test yourself

Vocabulary

1 Choose the correct word to complete the sentences.

1 Did you *clean* / *do* / *make* the house?
2 I usually *clean* / *do* / *make* the shopping at the weekend.
3 Can you help me *clean* / *do* / *make* dinner?
4 It's great to *clean* / *do* / *make* nothing on Sunday.
5 She often *cleans* / *does* / *makes* breakfast for the family.

/5

2 Look at the pictures and complete the sentences.

1 The shoes are *sixty-five euros*.

2 The newspaper is ________________.

3 The dance classes are ________________.

4 The camera is ________________.

5 The sunglasses are ________________.

6 The CDs are ________________.

/5

Grammar

3 Rearrange the words to make questions.

1 go out   you   Did ?

____

2 you   did   last night   What   do ?

____

3 at   Was   the quiz   Sandra ?

____

4 Sunday night   was   Where   on   Carl ?

____

5 enjoy   Did   the party   they ?

____

/5

4 Match the questions 1–5 in exercise 3 to the answers a–e.

☐ a Yes, they did.
☐ b Yes, she was.
☐ c No, I didn't.
☐ d I stayed at home and watched TV.
☐ e He was with his friends.

/5

Functional language

5 Put the missing words in the correct place in each sentence.

1 Can I *pay* by credit card?
2 Where the changing rooms?
3 How much this?
4 I'm just thanks.
5 Can help you?
6 Is twenty pounds, thanks.

/5

Total: /25

9 & 10 | Reading

1 Look at the photo. What city is it? How do you know?

1 New York, US 2 Dublin, Ireland 3 Cairo, Egypt

2 Read the article to check your answer to exercise 1.

St Patrick's Day

I'm from Dublin, the capital of Ireland. The population is 1.1 million. In Dublin we have a special holiday – St Patrick's Day. Every year we celebrate St Patrick's Day on 17th March. St Patrick is the patron saint of Ireland. Green is the colour of St Patrick's Day, and people usually wear something green on this day. All over the world Irish and non-Irish people celebrate this day.

Last year I was in New York for St Patrick's Day. It was on a Tuesday. There was a big parade in the city. The police said there were two million people on the streets. I drank lemonade and ate some green cheese. It was great. This is a photo of that day.

3 Read the article again and answer the questions.

1 Where is the writer from?

_______________________________________.

2 What day is St Patrick's Day?

_______________________________________.

3 What is the important colour for St Patrick's Day?

_______________________________________.

4 Where was the writer last year on St Patrick's Day?

_______________________________________.

5 What did the writer do?

_______________________________________.

READ & LISTEN

4 **41** Listen to Reading 9 & 10 *St Patrick's Day* on the CD and read the article again.

11A | Special people

Action verbs

1 Choose the correct verb to complete the sentences.

1 I can *drive* / *play* a car.
2 Can you *sing* / *dance* a song?
3 I often *type* / *play* video games.
4 Can you *type* / *dance* this letter?
5 I love to *dance* / *sing* salsa.

Can/can't

2 Write questions with *can* using the words in brackets.

1 'Our son is married to a French woman.' (*he / speak French*)
Can he speak French?

2 'I want to be in a rock band.' (*you / play guitar*)
____.

3 'He wants to work with computers.' (*he / type*)
____.

4 'My parents love the beach.' (*they / swim*)
____.

5 'She doesn't have an email address.' (*she / set one up*)
____.

6 'I'm taking piano lessons.' (*you / read music*)
____.

3 Complete the sentences with *can* or *can't*.

A: (1) __________ you speak French?
B: No, I (2) __________, but I (3) __________ speak Czech.

Ana Lucia (4) _____ play the violin, but she (5) ______ play the guitar.

Fred (6) ______ use a computer, but Mary (7) _____ use a computer.

I (8) _____ ski very well.

Dictation

4 **42** Write the sentences that you hear.

1 ____?
2 ____.
3 ____.
4 ____.

Read & listen

5 **43** Read and listen to the article *People look at us* on page 97 of the Student's Book.

11B | Special event

PRESENT CONTINUOUS

1 Put the verbs into the *-ing* form.

1 swim	________	5 play	________
2 run	________	6 make	________
3 eat	________	7 drive	________
4 talk	________	8 type	________

2 Complete the text with the present continuous of the verbs in brackets.

A: And now a special *Top Music* TV report from John Westley. John?

B: Yes, hello. I (1) __________ (*talk*) to you from Glastonbury.

A: How is the weather?

B: Well, today is a good day. It (2) __________ (*not rain*).

A: Is there any music at the moment? What (3) __________ the people (4) __________ (*do*)?

B: Two groups (5) __________ (*play*). People (6) __________ (*dance*) and there's a good atmosphere.

3 Write questions and answers in the present continuous using the prompts.

1 What / you / do — We / play / video games
A: What are you doing?
B: We're playing video games.

2 What / he / do — He / talk / with his boss
A: ________________________________?
B: ________________________________.

3 What / they / eat — They / eat / fish
A: ________________________________?
B: ________________________________.

4 Where / you / go — I / go / to class
A: ________________________________?
B: ________________________________.

5 What language / she / speak — She / speak / Thai
A: ________________________________?
B: ________________________________.

6 What / they / do — They / play / music
A: ________________________________?
B: ________________________________.

TRANSLATION

4 Translate the sentences into your language.

1 I'm talking on the phone.

________________________________.

2 What are you doing?

________________________________?

3 She's not listening.

________________________________.

4 Where are you going?

________________________________?

11c | Special paintings

Talking about a painting

1 Complete the text with the words from the box.

artist   paintings   art   photo

I really like (1) __________. My favourite (2) __________ is Van Gogh. I have two Van Gogh (3) __________ in my room. I like photography, too. This is a (4) __________ of some sunflowers. It's also in my room.

2 Rearrange the words to make sentences.

1 this picture see I a boat can in .

____

2 are women two There .

____

3 think I she sad is .

____

4 people dancing are The .

____

5 children Maybe the playing are .

____

3 Tick (✓) the correct sentence, a or b.

1 a) There are a girl in the painting. ____
  b) There is a girl in the painting. ✓

2 a) I think this is a British painting. ____
  b) I think this is a painting British. ____

3 a) I can see a man and a woman. ____
  b) Can I see a man and a woman. ____

4 a) Maybe are husband and wife. ____
  b) Maybe they are husband and wife. ____

5 a) They are on a boat and it raining. ____
  b) They are on a boat and it is raining. ____

Listening

4 **44** Listen to the dialogue and answer the questions.

1 Where is the artist from?

______________________________.

2 Does the woman like the painting?

______________________________.

3 Does the man like the painting?

______________________________.

Read & listen

5 **45** Read and listen to the article *Special paintings* on page 100 of the Student's Book.

11 Test yourself

Vocabulary

1 Write the verbs for the pictures.

1 to __________

2 to __________

3 to __________ the piano

4 to __________

5 to __________

/5

Grammar

2 Rearrange the words to make sentences.

1 swim I can't .

____

2 Thai She speak can .

____

3 me hear Can you ?

____

4 do can you What ?

____

5 the We teacher hear can't .

____

/5

3 Complete the sentences with the present continuous of the verbs in brackets.

1 **A**: Where are you?

B: I'm at home. I __________ (*watch*) TV.

2 **C**: You __________ (*not listen*) to me.

D: Yes, I am!

3 **E**: John is late for class.

F: Yes, he __________ (*run*) for the bus now.

4 **G**: What __________ they __________ (*talk*) about?

H: Their holiday in Kenya.

5 **I**: Can you talk now?

J: No, I can't. The concert __________ (*start*).

/5

4 Tick (✓) the correct answer, a or b.

1 Do you like the painting?
- a) Yes, I do. ____
- b) Yes, I like. ____

2 Can he speak English?
- a) Yes, he cans. ____
- b) Yes, he can. ____

3 Can you spell your name?
- a) No, I don't. ____
- b) No, I can't. ____

4 Is it raining?
- a) Yes, it is. ____
- b) Yes, it does. ____

5 Do they work here?
- a) No, they do. ____
- b) No, they don't. ____

/5

Functional language

5 Complete the sentences 1–5 with the phrases a–e.

1 You can also see some
2 This painting is
3 There's a woman
4 They are drinking
5 The small boat

- ☐ a in the painting.
- ☐ b one of the most popular in Britain.
- ☐ c is pulling the big boat.
- ☐ d children in the painting.
- ☐ e and having a good time.

/5

Total: /25

12A | The phone

Telephoning

1 Complete the phrases 1–5 with the words and phrases a–e.

1 Can I ☐ a to call back?
2 Is Susan ☐ b a message?
3 I'm sorry, ☐ c speak to John Smith?
4 Can I take ☐ d she isn't here.
5 Would you like ☐ e there?

2 Complete the two dialogues with the phrases from exercise 1. There is one extra phrase.

1

A: Hello.

B: Hello. 914 5124.

A: (1) ______________________________?

B: Susan?

A: Yes, Susan Harper.

B: Oh, Susan. No, (2) ______________________.

2

A: John Smith's office.

B: (3) ______________________________?

A: I'm sorry, he's in a meeting. (4) ____________ ______________________________?

B: Yes. Can you tell him Jake Rollins phoned?

A: Certainly, sir.

Telephone English

3 Choose the correct word or phrase to complete the sentences.

1 Can you *call / turn on / send* me on 07941935? Thanks.
2 When you *turn off / turn on / send* your phone, enter the PIN code.
3 Write a message and press *turn off / call / send*.

Listening

4 **46** Listen and complete the voicemail messages.

1 Hi Sara, (1) _______ Mum. (2) _______ _______ at home.
2 I'm sorry, Jason (3) _______ _______.
3 Please leave (4) _______ _______ and I'll call (5) _______ _______.
4 This is 0741293. I'm sorry, I (6) _______ _______ your call.
5 Hi, (7) _______ _______ Phil. Can you call me on (8) _______? Thanks.

Translation

5 Translate the sentences into your language.

1 Is that Mrs Hill?
______________________________?
2 I'm sorry, she isn't here.
______________________________.
3 Can I take a message?
______________________________?
4 Would you like to call back?
______________________________?
5 Please tell her I called.
______________________________.

Read & listen

6 **47** Read and listen to the article *Me and my mobile* on page 104 of the Student's Book.

12B | The airport

AT THE AIRPORT

1 Find six words about the airport in the wordsearch.

A	W	D	E	L	A	Y	E	D
Z	Q	E	H	L	E	E	G	S
B	P	P	A	E	R	L	R	F
N	R	A	R	R	I	V	A	L
V	K	R	E	D	D	O	E	I
X	T	T	B	T	O	V	N	G
M	P	U	G	E	T	E	T	H
Y	I	R	E	W	Z	P	S	T
C	H	E	C	K	I	N	U	O
L	C	C	U	S	T	O	M	S

GOING TO (1) FUTURE PLANS

2 Write questions using the prompts.

1 What / you / do

What are you going to do?

2 Where / he / fly

Where is he going to fly?

3 Where / you / travel

____________________?

4 What / she / see

____________________?

5 Where / they / stay

____________________?

6 Who / you / visit

____________________?

7 When / he / leave

____________________?

3 Rearrange the words to make sentences or questions.

1 my visit going to I'm friends .

____

2 going to fly you Are ?

____

3 not No, I'm fly going to .

____

4 travel are How going to you ?

____

5 drive I'm my car going to .

____

4 Make sentences with *going to* and the words in brackets.

1 I'm __________ (*not fly*).

2 She's __________ (*buy a ticket*).

3 They're __________ (*not visit London*).

4 I'm __________ (*take a photo*).

5 We're __________ (*not say goodbye*).

DICTATION

5 **48** Write the sentences that you hear.

1 ____________________.

2 ____________________?

3 ____________________?

4 ____________________.

12c | The end

Feelings

1 Rearrange the letters to make words and complete the sentences.

1 She's _____ (asd) because school is going to finish.
2 They're _____ (ppyha) because they're eating ice cream.
3 I'm _____ (irted) because I worked hard today.
4 He's _____ (crased) because he doesn't like dogs.
5 She's _____ (grany) because her son is dirty.

Best wishes for the future

2 Look at the alphabetti-spaghetti and find four expressions.

haveagoodweekend seeyoutomorrowmorninggoodluckwithyourexamgoodbye

Going to (2); future time expressions

3 Rearrange the letters to make words and complete the sentences.

1 Are you going to come to the party _______ (ithotgn)?
2 We're going to see a film ________ (wrotroom venigen).
3 _______ (motrowor) we're going to have our last lesson.
4 She's going to visit her family ________ (xetn thonm).
5 Are you going to study English ________ (exnt ryea)?

4 Correct one mistake in each sentence or question.

1 Where you going to go tonight?
2 Is he going come here next week?
3 What are you going to tomorrow do?
4 I'm not to see her tonight.
5 I'm next year going to study English again.

Listening

5 **49** Listen and write *M* (for the man) or *W* (for the woman) to complete the sentences.

1 The ____ is going to go to Thailand.
2 The ____ is going to visit some friends.
3 The ____ is not going to go on holiday.
4 The ____ is going to paint his house.
5 The ____ is going to send a postcard.

Read & listen

6 **50** Read and listen to the blog *The end of the course!* on page 108 of the Student's Book.

12 | Test yourself

Functional language

1 Complete the sentences with the words from the box.

tell	call	take	speak	isn't

1 Can I __________ to Jim?

2 I'm sorry. Jim __________ here.

3 Would you like to __________ back?

4 Can I __________ a message?

5 Please __________ him I called.

/5

Vocabulary

2 Complete the sentences with the words or phrases from the box.

call	happy	send	tired	turn off

1 I often __________ text messages to my friends.

2 I feel __________ when my best friend calls me.

3 Please __________ your phone when the class starts.

4 I'm sorry, I can't answer the phone now. Leave a message and I'll __________ you back.

5 A: You look really __________.

B: I know, I need to go to sleep.

/5

Grammar

3 Write questions with *going to* using the prompts.

1 you / go on holiday

____?

2 When / you / travel

____?

3 he / see his friends

____?

4 they / do the shopping tomorrow

____?

5 What / she / do tonight

____?

/10

4 Complete the dialogue with *going to* and the verb in brackets. Use contractions where possible.

J: Hi, Bobby! What are you (1) __________ (*do*) tonight?

B: Hi, Julie! I (2) __________ (*see*) a film. Would you like to come?

J: No, thanks. I (3) __________ (*study*).

B: I (4) __________ (*not study*).

J: But we (5) __________ (*have*) an exam tomorrow!

B: I know.

J: Well, good luck!

/5

Total: /25

11 & 12 | Reading

1 Read the two postcards. Where are Tomas and Sandra?

Dear Kati,
Here's another postcard from our school trip to Britain! I'm here with Kerry and Matt. This place is fantastic. We arrived on Monday and stayed in the hotel. Yesterday we went to the town centre. We walked around the cathedral. It's next to the castle and it's very British! I loved it. Tonight, there's a free concert in Castle Square. It's going to be great. Tomorrow we're going to the theatre. Anyway, I'm having a good time. You wouldn't like it here – there isn't a beach!
Bye.
Sandra

Kati N
Rue d
Paris
France

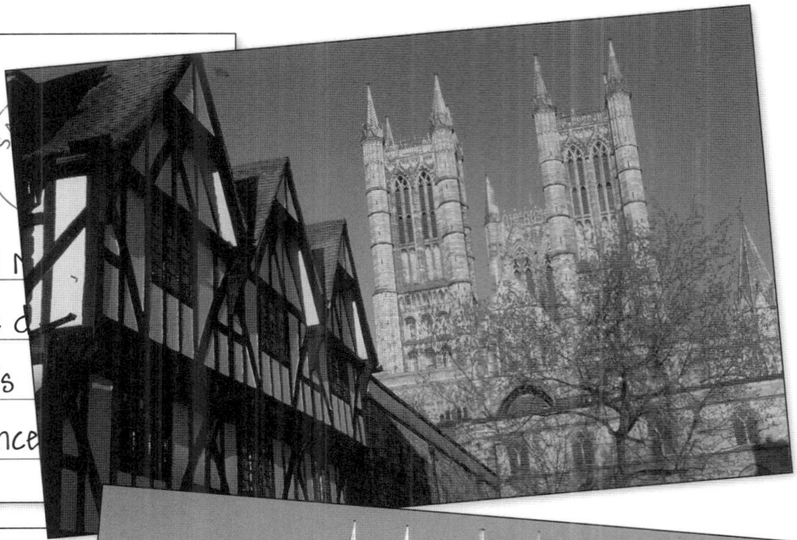

Hi Mum,
How are you? This postcard is from Lincoln. It's a small city in Britain. The cathedral is great, but I don't like the city very much. I'm here for the weekend. The weather today is awful; cold and grey. I'm at a good hotel in the city centre. The other problem is I don't have my car here, and you know I hate public transport! Last night we had dinner in a restaurant and I walked back to the hotel, in the rain! Tomorrow, I'm going to be at the conference for the day. Maybe I can phone you then. Anyway, hope you are well.
Love Tomas

LINCOLN
Mum & Da
Budapest
Hungary

2 Read the postcards again. Choose the correct answer, a, b or c.

1 _____ likes the city.
a) Kati.
b) Sandra.
c) Tomas.

2 _____ thinks the cathedral is great.
a) Kati.
b) Sandra.
c) Tomas.

3 Where is the cathedral?
a) Next to the castle.
b) Next to the hotel.
c) Next to the theatre.

4 Who is staying in Lincoln on Saturday and Sunday?
a) Kerry and Matt.
b) Sandra.
c) Tomas.

5 Where is Tomas going to go tomorrow?
a) The cathedral.
b) A conference.
c) The theatre.

6 Why did Sandra like the cathedral?
a) It's very British.
b) It's big.
c) You can walk around it.

Read & listen

3 **51** Listen to Reading 11 & 12 *Postcards* on the CD and read the postcards again.

1 | WRITING Completing a form

READING

1 Read the online form and answer the questions.

File Edit View Favourites Tools Help Link

www.hotels2go.col

(1) Mr ☑ **(2) Mrs** ☐ **(3) Ms** ☐
Last name(s): Roberts
First name: Frank
(4) Address: 36 Cambridge St
City: Manchester
Country: United Kingdom
Telephone number:
Home: 44 603 295 4565
Work: 44 603 340 2323
Mobile: 44 600 095 743
Email: froberts@ukmail.col
Name of hotel: Hotel Star **City:** Berlin
(5) Single room ☑
(6) Double room ☐

1 Where is he from?

______________________________________.

2 Where is his hotel?

______________________________________.

3 What is his home telephone number?

______________________________________.

4 What's his last name?

______________________________________.

2 Look at the highlighted words in the online form in exercise 1. What are they in your language?

1 ____________
2 ____________
3 ____________
4 ____________
5 ____________
6 ____________

LANGUAGE FOCUS

3 Read the information in the box.

Useful language

In English, these words start with a CAPITAL letter:

First names and last names:	*John, Margaret, Smith*
Countries and cities:	*Japan, Italy, Germany, Paris*
Street and place names:	*Oxford Street, Fifth Avenue, Regent Hotel*
The first word in a sentence:	*This is my teacher.*
The pronoun *I*:	*He's from Germany and I'm from Canada.*
Titles:	*Mr, Mrs, Ms*

4 Rewrite the text with capital letters.

my name is frank roberts and i'm from manchester. i'm in the hotel star in berlin, in germany.

WRITING

5 Complete the form for the Regent Hotel in London with your information.

File Edit View Favourites Tools Help Link

www.hotels2go.col

Mr ☐ **Mrs** ☐ **Ms** ☐
Last name(s):
First name:
Address:
City:
Country:
Telephone number:
Home:
Work:
Mobile:
Email:
Name of hotel:
City:
Single room ☐
Double room ☐

2 | Writing A paragraph about you

Reading

1 Read the text and decide if the sentences are true (T) or false (F). Correct the false sentences.

What about you?

My name is Costas Tamami. I'm a taxi driver and a student. I'm from Thessaloniki, Greece. I'm Greek-American. My father is from Greece. His name is Luke. My mother's name is Cindy. She's from Las Vegas in the US. My wife's name is Sandra. She's from Germany. My English class is on Monday and Wednesday. What about you?

1 His name is Costas. ____
2 He's a teacher. ____
3 His father is from the US. ____
4 His mother is American. ____
5 His wife is from Britain. ____
6 He has English class two days in the week. ____

Language focus

2 Read the information in the box.

Useful language

Punctuation

capital letter	P
full stop	.
apostrophe	'
question mark	?

capital letter – days of the week
capital letter – nationalities
capital letter – start of a sentence
full stop – end of a sentence
apostrophe – contractions and possessives
question mark – end of a question

3 Correct the punctuation in the sentences.

1 What's your name?
2 My wifes name is jenny.
3 Shes from germany
4 Her parents are teachers. Theyre german teachers.
5 Their classes are on tuesday and thursday.

Writing

4 Write a paragraph about you. Answer the questions.

What's your name?
Where are you from?
Where are your parents from?
What do you do?
When is your English class?

3 | WRITING A person you know

READING

1 Read the text and complete the sentences with a word.

This is a photo of my sister, Natasha. Natasha's British, but she has a Russian name because our mother is from Russia. Natasha's 20 years old. She doesn't go to school. She works in an office in London. It's a good job, but she doesn't like it very much. Natasha and I like Italian food, and we listen to British and American music. I see Natasha every week. Natasha and I are sisters, but we are also friends.

1 Natasha is the writer's ______________.
2 Natasha doesn't go to ______________.
3 Natasha's mother is from ______________.
4 Natasha ______________ like her job.
5 The writer sees Natasha every ______________.

LANGUAGE FOCUS

2 Complete the sentences with *and* or *but*.

1 Her name's Natasha __________ she's 20.
2 She has a job, __________ she doesn't like it.
3 She's a personal assistant __________ she works in an office.
4 She works in an office, __________ I don't. I work in a factory.

3 Choose the correct word to complete the rules.

1 We use *and* / *but* when two ideas go together.
2 We use *and* / *but* when one idea is different from the other idea in a sentence.

WRITING

4 Choose a person you know and write a text about her/him.

Useful language

Age:	*She/He is … years old.*
Job:	*She/He is a/an …*
Origin:	*She/He is from …*
Likes:	*She/He likes … and …*
Free time:	*She/He … in her/his free time.*

4 | WRITING A city description

READING

1 Read the article about San Francisco and answer the questions.

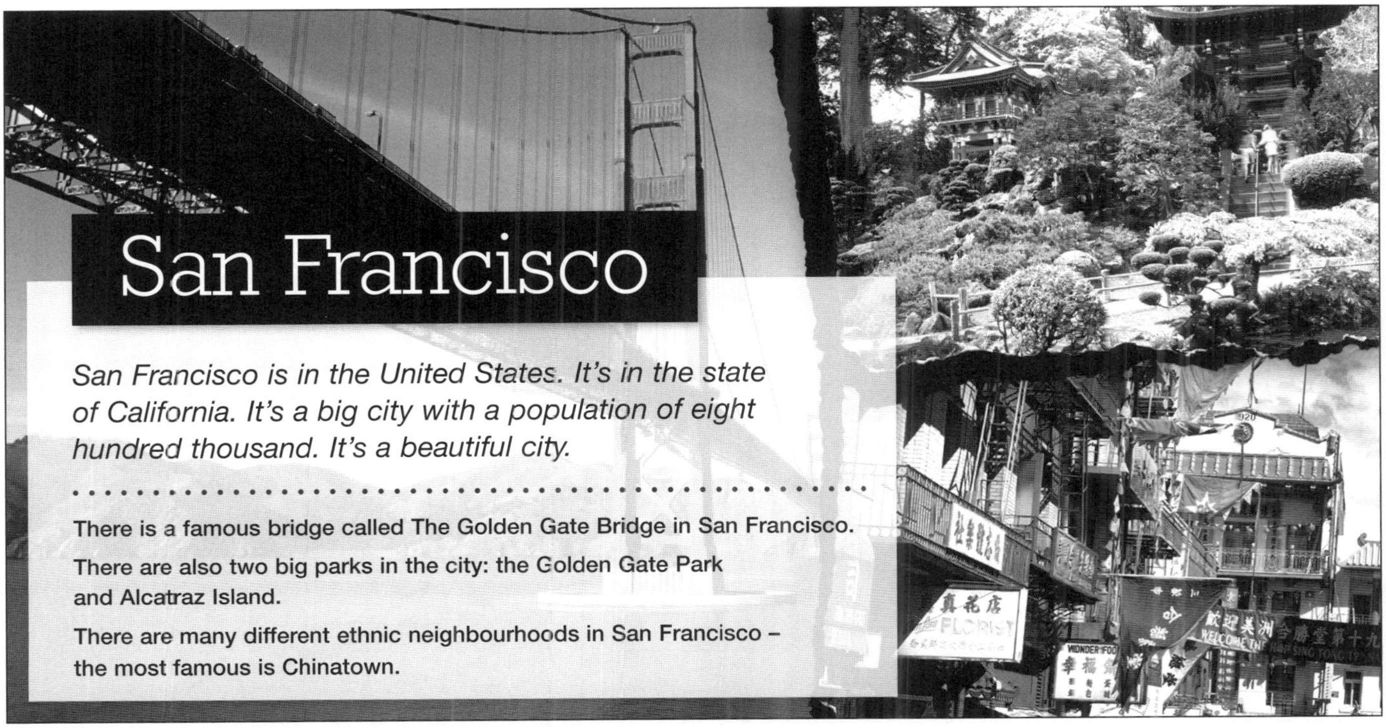

San Francisco

San Francisco is in the United States. It's in the state of California. It's a big city with a population of eight hundred thousand. It's a beautiful city.

There is a famous bridge called The Golden Gate Bridge in San Francisco.

There are also two big parks in the city: the Golden Gate Park and Alcatraz Island.

There are many different ethnic neighbourhoods in San Francisco – the most famous is Chinatown.

1 What's the population of San Francisco?

______________________________.

2 Are there any parks in the city?

______________________________.

3 What's the name of the bridge?

______________________________.

4 What's the most famous neighbourhood in San Francisco?

______________________________.

LANGUAGE FOCUS

2 Read the information in the box.

Useful language

A paragraph
Start (sentence 1): This sentence gives the main idea of the paragraph. It is the first sentence.
Middle (sentences 2 and any further ones): These sentences come after the topic sentence and give more information and details.
End (final sentence): This sentence comes at the end of the paragraph.

3 Label the sentences Start (*S*), Middle (*M*) or End (*E*).

a ☐ There are two small parks in the city centre and there is a castle. ___

b ☐ It's a small city with a population of 300,000. ___

c ☐ Nottingham is an interesting place to visit. ___

d ☐ Nottingham is in Britain. ___

e ☐ There is a statue of Robin Hood. ___

4 Put the sentences from exercise 3 in the correct order to make a paragraph.

WRITING

5 Write a paragraph about a city you know.

5 | WRITING A holiday blog

READING

1 Read the blog and answer the questions.

File Edit View Favourites Tools Help Links »

Mary's holiday

The holiday in Marrakech was great.
We arrived on Tuesday. First we went shopping in the market and I bought a beautiful teapot. On Tuesday we visited an old castle. Then we ate lunch in a café. It was very hot in the afternoon. We went to the hotel to sleep first. Then in the evening we went to the main square and listened to the music. There were lots of people and it was very noisy.

1 Where did Mary go on holiday?

____.

2 What did she buy?

____.

3 Where did she have lunch?

____.

4 What did she do in the evening?

____.

LANGUAGE FOCUS

2 Read the information in the box.

Useful language

Using linkers: *first & then*
Use *first* and *then* to show a sequence of events.
***First** we went shopping …*
***Then** we ate lunch in a café.*
*We went back to the hotel to sleep **first**. **Then** in the evening we went to the main square.*

- ***First*** can go at the beginning or end of a sentence.
- ***Then*** goes at the beginning of a sentence.

3 Complete the blog with *first* or *then*.

File Edit View Favourites Tools Help Link

We arrived at the hotel at eight o'clock in the morning. (1) __________ we went to our room. (2) __________ we went swimming in the hotel pool. In the evening we walked around the city. We visited the shops (3) __________,
(4) __________ we ate dinner in a lovely restaurant.
We arrived back at the hotel at ten o'clock.
It was a very good day.

WRITING

4 Write your own holiday blog.

6 | WRITING A letter asking for information

READING

1 Match the advertisements A–C to the letters 1–2. There is one extra advertisement.

A

ENGLISH LANGUAGE COURSE SUMMER SPECIAL
We have courses in Dublin, London and Edinburgh.
Stay with a British family and enjoy cultural visits.
Email: summercourse@english_in_britain.co.ur

B

HOLIDAY HOUSE in SPAIN
July and/or August
Email: David Holmes dholmes@mailfrance.nxt

C

ENGLISH BOOK FAIR
A great collection of books.
London October 3–6.
For more information contact
info@londonenglishbooks.co.ur

1 ☐

Dear Mr Holmes,
I'm writing about your advertisement for a holiday house in Spain. It was in the *Sunday Globe* newspaper. Can you give me more information about the price and location?
Thank you very much.
Yours sincerely,
Jamie Bennett

2 ☐

Dear Sir or Madam,
I saw an advertisement about the English Book Fair in October and I'd like some more information. I'm going to be in London on October 4th. Can you tell me the address?
Yours faithfully,
Helga Emmerson

LANGUAGE FOCUS

2 Complete the phrases.

Beginning a letter

(1) __________ | Mr Holmes/Mrs Holmes,*
| Sir (2) __________ Madam,**

Asking for information

I (3) __________

writing (4) __________ | your advertisement.
| the job.
| the house for sale.

I'd (5) __________ some (6) __________ information.

Could | you give me | some information (7) __________ the price/location?
Can | | the details?
| | the address?

Ending a letter

Thanks. (8) __________ | sincerely,*
| faithfully,**

WRITING

3 Write a letter asking for more information about the extra advertisement. Ask about:

- price.
- location.
- dates.

Use the expressions in exercise 2 to help you.

Language note:
* This is formal use if you know the name of the person.
** This is formal use if you don't know the name of the person.

Audioscripts

1B Greetings exercise 5 1

W = woman M = man
M: Hello. I'm Max.
W: Hello, Max. My name's Victoria.
M: Nice to meet you.
W: Nice to meet you, too.

1B Listening exercise 6 2

W = woman M = man
W: Where are you from, Max?
M: I'm from Germany.
W: Germany! Mmm. I'm from the United States ... Los Angeles.
M: Ah. Very nice.

2A Listening exercise 5 4

R = receptionist W1 = woman 1 M1 = man 1
W2 = woman 2 M2 = man 2

1 **R:** What's your name?
W1: Carol Byrd.
R: How do you spell your last name?
W1: B-Y-R-D.

2 **R:** What's your name?
M1: John Heart.
R: How do you spell your last name?
M1: H-E-A-R-T.

3 **R:** What's your name?
M2: Mr and Mrs Jons.
R: How do you spell your name?
M2: J-O-N-S.

4 **R:** What's your name?
W2: Jane Puts.
R: How do you spell your last name?
W2: P-U-T-S.

2 Test yourself Listening exercise 5 6

C = customer W = waitress
C: Excuse me. I'd like a coffee, please.
W: Would you like black or white?
C: Black, please.
W: Here you are.
C: Thank you.

3A Listening exercise 5 8

1 She's a doctor. Her name's Samantha.
2 They're from New York. They're police officers.
3 She's Amy. She's an aid worker.
4 I'm a teacher. I'm from London.

4B Listening exercise 3 13

1
W1 = woman 1 M = man W2 = woman 2
W1: Hi, Bryan!
M: Hello, Katie! How are you?
W1: Fine, thanks. Bryan, this is ...
W2: Hello, my name's Rachel.
M: Oh, are you Katie's sister?
W2: No, no.
W1: Rachel is my mother.
W2: Nice to meet you, Bryan.

2
W = woman M = man
W: What's this photo?
M: This one? My parents.
W: Wow. They're so young. Is this Rome?
M: Yes, it is. I'm from Britain, but my mother is from Italy.

3
W1 = woman 1 W2 = woman 2
W1: How are you, Doris?
W2: I'm fine.
W1: How is your son? What's his name again?
W2: Oh, you mean Jeffrey? He's fine.
W1: Ah, good.
W2: Yes, do you know ... he's eighteen years old now.
W1: Eighteen?
W2: Yes, he's not my baby boy anymore.

5A Listening exercise 5 16

My name's Thomas Martin. I'm from London, but I live in Sydney, Australia now. I work in an office here in Sydney. I'm married. My wife's name is Jenny. She works in a school. She goes to school by bus. She's from Australia.

6C Listening exercise 4 22

I = interviewer W = woman
I: Excuse me. I'm doing a survey on habits. Can I ask you some questions?
W: Yes, OK.
I: What's your name?
W: Frances.
I: What time do you usually wake up in the morning, Frances?
W: Oh! I always wake up early, at half past six.
I: Wow, that is early. Do you drink coffee in the morning?
W: No, never. I drink orange juice and eat toast.
I: How often do you eat meat and fish?
W: I never eat meat, but I eat fish twice a week.
I: And how often do you eat with your family?
W: Oh ..., with my parents, about once a month.
I: And how often do you go to bed after twelve o'clock?
W: Well, I work every day, so I usually go to bed early, but I go to bed late on Friday and Saturday. So, twice a week.
I: Thank you.

7B Listening exercise 5 25

W = woman M = man
M: Hello.
W: Hi, my name's Roberta.
M: Oh. Hello.
W: I live next to you. I'm the new person in the building.
M: Nice to meet you.
W: Nice to meet you, too. Is it OK if I ask you some questions about the neighbourhood?
M: Sure. OK.
W: Is there a supermarket? To buy some food?
M: Yes, there is. Do you have a map?
W: Yes, I do. Here.
M: OK, look. The supermarket is here and all the good shops are here.
W: OK. Great! Thank you very much.
M: You're welcome.
W: Bye bye!
M: Goodbye.

7c Listening exercise 1 26

AW = American woman SM = Spanish man
AW: Excuse me! Where's the cathedral?
SM: Can you repeat, please?
AW: Where's the cathedral?
SM: I'm sorry. I don't understand.
AW: Oh! Do you speak English?
SM: No, I don't speak English.
AW: Oh!
SM: Do you speak Spanish?
AW: No, I don't.

8b Listening exercise 5 30

K = Kellerman J = Janet D = Diaz
K: Hello. Please sit down. We have some questions for you.
J: OK.
D: What's your name? Just for the record ...
J: My name is Janet Smith.
K: Are you Mr John Magnus' ex-wife?
J: Yes, I am. We were married for ten years.
D: What was your relationship with Peter Gordon?
J: We were friends. Only friends. But not now.
K: Hmm. Yeah.
J: I wasn't in love with Peter, if that's what you mean.
D: Excuse me, can you repeat that, please?
J: I wasn't in love with Peter. He is – sorry, was – a bad man.
D: Was Peter with you last night?
J: No, he wasn't.
D: Was he at the factory?
J: I don't know. I was.
D: Really?
J: Yes, it was me. I started the fire.

9a Listening exercise 4 32

B = Bob S = Sandie R = Richard H = Holly
1 **B:** Last year I went to ... on holiday. I saw the Pantheon and I ate moussaka. It was fantastic.
2 **S:** Last year we went on holiday to ... I went swimming in the sea and I ate paella. I loved it.
3 **R:** I went on holiday to ... I went to Disney World and I saw the White House.
4 **H:** I went to ... with my boyfriend. We saw the Taj Mahal and drank chai. I enjoyed it.

9b Listening exercise 4 34

W1 = woman 1 M = man W2 = woman 2
W1: My name is Shaheena. In 1969 I was six years old so I don't remember much about the sixties. We had a radio, but we didn't listen to the Beatles.
M: I was eighteen in 1969 and I went to Woodstock with my friends. It was a big concert with 450,000 people. Bob Dylan and Jimi Hendrix played.
W2: I wasn't born in 1969, but my parents always talked about the day Neil Armstrong landed on the moon. They didn't have a television, but they watched the Apollo landing at a friend's house.

10a Listening exercise 4 37

1
C = Carole J = Jenny
C: Hi, Jenny. Did you have a good weekend?
J: Yes, I went to the cinema with Mike.
C: Really? What did you see?
J: The new *Superman* film.
C: That sounds great.

2
J = Jane L = Louise
J: Hi, Louise. What time did you get home last night?
L: I didn't get home.
J: Why? What happened?
L: I missed the bus.
J: Oh no!

3
M1 = man 1 M2 = man 2
M1: What did you do at the weekend?
M2: I went to that new Chinese restaurant.
M1: Was it good?
M2: Yes, it was. It was great.

11c Listening exercise 4 44

W = woman M = man
W: Oh, look at this one.
M: Mmm. Who is the artist?
W: Diego Rivera. He's a Mexican artist.
M: I know Diego Rivera. Do you like it?
W: The painting?
M: Yes.
W: Mmm. Yes, I do.
M: Oh.
W: What do you think?
M: I don't know. I don't like it very much.
W: But it's beautiful.
M: I know ... it's just ... I don't like art.
W: Oh.

12a Listening exercise 4 46

1 Hi Sara, it's Mum. Call me at home.
2 I'm sorry, Jason isn't here.
3 Please leave a message and I'll call you back.
4 This is 0741293. I'm sorry, I can't answer your call.
5 Hi, this is Phil. Can you call me on 0712665? Thanks.

12c Listening exercise 5 49

A = Andy J = Jane
A: What are you going to do next week?
J: I'm going to travel to Thailand.
A: Thailand?
J: Yes, I'm going to visit some friends.
A: Wow!
J: What about you?
A: I'm not going to go on holiday. I'm going to stay at home.
J: Really?
A: Yes, I'm going to paint my house.
J: Well, I'm going to send you a postcard.
A: Thanks. That's nice.

The Black Tulip

A Note About This Story

Time: 1671 to 1673. **Place:** The Netherlands.

In the middle of the nineteenth century, Alexandre Dumas heard two interesting stories about the Netherlands. They were stories about the Netherlands in the seventeenth century. Then Dumas himself wrote a novel about the Netherlands in the 1670s. He put the two interesting stories into his new novel.

One of these stories was about two brothers, John and Cornelius De Witt. The brothers lived in The Hague in the seventeenth century. They were officials in the government of the Dutch Republic.

At that time, the Netherlands belonged to two countries. The area in the south had belonged to Spain for many years. This was the Spanish Netherlands. But France wanted this land, and in 1668, France took a large part of the land. Today, most of this area is called Belgium. The area in the north was the Dutch Republic. Seven states were joined in this republic. These states were Holland, Zeeland, Utrecht, Gelderland, Friesland, Groningen and Overijssl. The Dutch Republic was often called the Seven States. Today, this area is sometimes called Holland and it is sometimes called the Netherlands. The Hague was the capital city of the Seven States.

In the 1670s, there was trouble in the Seven States. Many people wanted a new ruler. Earlier, the ruler of the Seven States had been the Stadtholder. But there had not been a Stadtholder for some years. In the 1670s, some people wanted a new Stadtholder. They wanted William, Prince of Orange. But other people did not want a Stadtholder – they wanted a king. They wanted King Louis XIV of France.

John and Cornelius De Witt did not want a new Stadtholder. They were against the Prince of Orange. But most of the people wanted a new government. They put the De Witts in prison. On 27th August 1672, a crowd of angry people murdered the brothers. And in 1672, William, Prince of Orange, became Stadtholder of the Dutch Republic.

From 1672 to 1678, the Republic was at war with France and England. The French army fought the Dutch army. There were battles on land and in ships at sea. In 1677, William of Orange married an English princess. In 1689, William became King of England, Scotland and Ireland and he moved to Britain.

In the seventeenth century, many people in the Netherlands grew tulips. The first tulips were brought to the Netherlands from Turkey in 1571. Soon, everybody in the Netherlands loved the flowers. Everybody wanted tulips. Stories, songs and poems were written about tulips.

The land in the Netherlands is good. Tulips grow well there. From the seventeenth century, thousands of Dutch people grew tulips. They grew tulips in the ground, in the spring. In the summer, they took the tulip bulbs out of the ground. They put the bulbs in drying-rooms. Then, the people planted their bulbs in the ground in the winter. The flowers grew again in the spring.

Tulip flowers are many different colours. In the seventeenth century, many people tried to grow black tulips. There was going to be a big prize for the grower of the first black tulip.

In the 1840s, Dumas read about the De Witts. And he heard stories about tulips in the Netherlands. Then he wrote a romantic adventure story. He called the story, *The Black Tulip*.

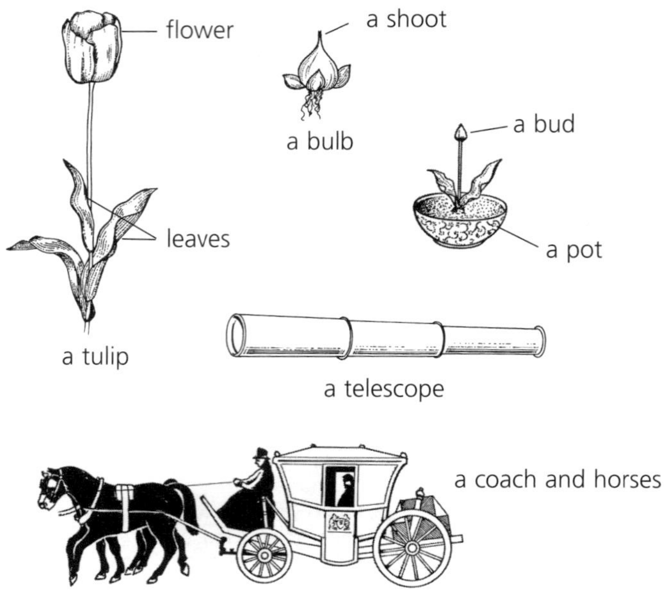

Note: Master = Mr

The People in This Story

Cornelius Van Baerle
kɔːœneɪlɪjəs fɒn 'bɑːlə

Isaac Boxtel
'aɪzæk 'bɒkstəl

Cornelius De Witt
kɔːœneɪlɪjəs də vɪt

John De Witt
dʒɒn də vɪt

Gryphus
'grɪfəs

Rosa
'rəʊsə

Craeke
'kreɪkə

William, Prince of Orange
wɪljəm, prɪns əv 'ɒrɪndʒ

Van Systens
fɒn 'sɪstəns

1 *Two Tulip-growers*

It was November 1671. Men in all the towns in the Seven States were reading this notice. Two of these men lived in the town of Dort. Their names were Isaac Boxtel and Cornelius Van Baerle.

Cornelius Van Baerle was a young man. He was twenty-five years old. He was very clever and he was very rich. He loved flowers. And he loved tulips more than all the other flowers. He grew beautiful tulips.

Cornelius Van Baerle was rich but he worked very hard. He built a special room with very big windows. This was his drying-room. Cornelius grew tulips in his garden. In the summer, he kept the tulip bulbs in his drying-room. In this special room, there were many drawers and cupboards.

'Can I grow a black tulip?' Cornelius asked himself. 'Yes! I have grown dark-blue tulips. I have grown dark-red tulips. Now I will grow a black tulip! It will be very difficult. But I will win the prize.'

'Yes, I will win 100,000 guilders,' Cornelius said to himself. 'But I don't want all the prize money. I will give 50,000 guilders to the poor people of Dort. Then I will travel. I will look for more tulips.'

Cornelius Van Baerle and Isaac Boxtel were neighbours. But they were not friends. Isaac was jealous of Cornelius.

'I hate Cornelius Van Baerle,' Isaac said to himself. 'Why does he grow tulips? He is a scientist. He is very rich. He doesn't want more money!'

Isaac Boxtel was an old man. He had a thin face and white hair. He was the best tulip-grower in Dort. He had been a tulip-grower for many years. He had grown many beautiful tulips.

'I have never seen a black tulip,' Isaac said to himself. 'But I will try to win this prize. I will try to grow a black tulip. I am a poor man. I want to win 100,000 guilders.'

'Cornelius Van Baerle has grown many beautiful tulips,' Isaac thought. 'But he has never grown a black tulip! I will grow a black tulip and I will win the prize. Then I will be rich, too.'

Every day, Isaac Boxtel saw Cornelius working in his garden. One day, Isaac bought a telescope. After that, he could watch Cornelius in his drying-room, too.

In that winter of 1671, Cornelius Van Baerle was working very hard. He was trying to grow a black tulip!

2 *The Package*

One day, Cornelius Van Baerle had a visitor – a man. The man's name was Cornelius De Witt. Cornelius De Witt was a very important man. He was an official of the government of the Seven States.

Cornelius' brother, John De Witt, was an important man, too. He was the leader of the government of the Seven States.

The De Witt brothers lived in The Hague – the capital city of the Seven States. But Cornelius De Witt owned a house in Dort, too. And Cornelius De Witt was Cornelius Van Baerle's guardian. The young man's father was dead.

The two men met one evening in January 1672. They met at Cornelius Van Baerle's house in Dort. Cornelius De Witt talked about politics. He talked about his brother, John – the leader of the government of the Seven States.

'I am sorry, sir,' young Cornelius said. 'I am not interested in politics. I am interested in tulips. Please, come to my drying-room. I will show you my bulbs.'

Isaac Boxtel was watching Van Baerle's house through his telescope. He saw some lights in Cornelius' drying-room – the lights from candles. Then Isaac saw the two men in the drying-room. He saw them, but he could not hear them speaking.

Isaac saw Cornelius De Witt give a package to the young man.

Young Cornelius did not open the package. He put it carefully in a drawer. Soon, the two men left the room.

'There are secrets in that package,' Isaac said to himself. 'One day, those secrets will bring trouble to Cornelius Van Baerle.'

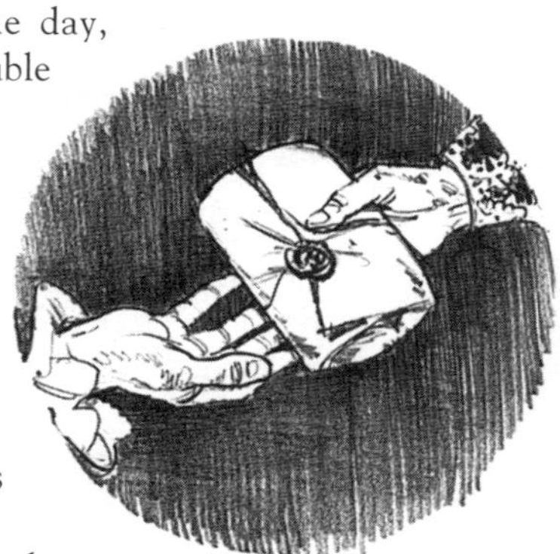

The next day, Cornelius De Witt returned to The Hague. And young Cornelius Van Baerle soon forgot about the package. Young Cornelius was not interested in the package. He was interested in his tulips.

For many months, Cornelius Van Baerle worked hard. In August, he had a large, special bulb. There were three small bulbs growing out of it.

The young man looked at the special bulb.

'These small bulbs will grow into black tulips. I am sure about that,' he said to himself.

He took the bulb to his drying-room. Carefully, he pulled the three small bulbs from the large bulb.

'Next spring, I will have a black tulip,' he thought. 'Today is the 20th August 1672. In November, I will plant these three small bulbs in the ground. Then, at the end of April 1673, I will have a black tulip!'

Test yourself checklist

Use this page to record your results from the *Test yourself* pages.
For example:

UNIT	Grammar	Vocabulary	Functional Language	Total Score /25
1	7/10	5/5	6/10	18

UNIT	Grammar	Vocabulary	Functional Language	Total Score /25
1				
2				
3				
4				
5				
6				
7				
8				
9				
10				
11				
12				
TOTAL				/300

Test yourself answer key

1 Test yourself

Functional language

1 1 Nice to meet you.
2 How are you?
3 What's your name?
4 This is Philip.
5 What's your phone number?

2 1 a 2 e 3 c 4 b 5 d

Grammar

3 1 is 2 is 3 am 4 are 5 is

4 1 a 2 a 3 a 4 b 5 a

Vocabulary

5 1 three 2 five 3 six 4 eight 5 ten

2 Test yourself

Vocabulary

1 1 twelve 2 thirteen 3 fifteen 4 sixteen
5 eighteen 6 twenty

2 1 key 2 lamp 3 sandwich 4 chair

Grammar

3 1 this 2 a 3 that 4 There 5 an

Functional language

4 1 What's your name?
2 How do you spell your name?
3 I'd like a croissant, please.
4 Would you like still or sparkling?
5 Would you like a coffee?

Listening

5 06

1 a coffee 2 Would you like 3 please
4 Here you 5 Thank

3 Test yourself

Vocabulary

1

job	country	nationality	colour	day
doctor	Brazil	French	blue	Friday
actor	China	German	yellow	Tuesday

2 1 France 2 Wednesday 3 green 4 French 5 diplomat

Grammar

3 1 isn't 2 are 3 'm 4 is 5 aren't

4 1 Where are you from?
2 Is she French?
3 What is your job?
4 Are you a police officer?
5 Is Yukiko from Japan?

Functional language

5 1 you do 2 your job 3 do you 4 don't 5 you on

4 Test yourself

Functional language

1 1 How old are you?
2 He's sixty-five years old.
3 It's a new computer.
4 How old are they?
5 He's a young man.

Vocabulary

2 1 It's a mobile phone.
2 It's a jacket.
3 It's an ID card.
4 It's money.
5 It's an umbrella.
6 It's a bag.

3 1 husband 2 brother 3 sister
4 parents 5 grandfather

Grammar

4 1 b 2 b 3 a 4 a 5 b

5 1 It 2 She 3 They 4 They 5 He

5 Test yourself

Vocabulary

1 1 factory 2 flat 3 foot 4 parents 5 bus

2 1 d 2 e 3 c 4 a 5 b

Grammar

3 1 He doesn't live in Germany.
2 He lives in Belgium.
3 Does she work in Beijing?
4 Do they go to school by bus?
5 He has a computer, but he doesn't use it.

4 1 Yes, they do.
2 Yes, they do.
3 No, she doesn't.
4 No, they don't.
5 Yes, he does.
6 Yes, they do.

Functional language

5 1 a 2 a 3 b 4 a 5 a

6 Test yourself

Vocabulary

1 1 c 2 f 3 d 4 b 5 a 6 e

2 1 salad D 2 fruit E 3 vegetables B
4 chicken A 5 toast C

Functional language

3 1 two o'clock 2 half past 3 to seven
4 quarter past 5 past twelve

Grammar

4 1 I always drink a cup of coffee in the morning.
2 He is often tired in the evening.
3 They usually go to work at nine o'clock.
4 Pete and Sally sometimes play tennis on Saturday afternoon.
5 I am never late for class.

5 1 c 2 d 3 a 4 e 5 b

7 Test yourself

Functional language

1 1 I don't understand.
2 Do you speak Chinese?
3 Can you repeat, please?
4 I only speak a little English.
5 I don't speak English.

Vocabulary

2 1 This is my flat. I live here with two friends. It's not very big and it's ugly. It's not a good flat, but it's cheap.
2 ugly
3 cheap
4 good
5 big

Grammar

3 1 There are 80 rooms.
2 There is a café.
3 There is wifi in every room.
4 There are three meeting rooms.
5 There are two restaurants.
6 There is an indoor swimming pool.

4 1 Is 2 isn't 3 are 4 Is 5 are

8 Test yourself

Functional language

1 1 b 2 a 3 a 4 c 5 c

Vocabulary

2 1 b 2 b 3 a 4 a 5 b

Grammar

3 1 was 2 was 3 were 4 weren't
5 was 6 were

4 1 I was at work last night.
2 Where were you yesterday?
3 It wasn't a good film.
4 Who was that man?
5 They weren't from France.

5 1 them 2 She 3 him 4 him 5 me

9 Test yourself

Vocabulary

1 1 hundred 2 million 3 thousand
4 hundred 5 thousand

2 1 September 2 February 3 December
4 July 5 April

Functional language

3 1 fourth of July 2 first of May
3 sixth of November 4 third of January
5 twenty-first of June 6 twelfth of August

Grammar

4 1 went 2 didn't see 3 had 4 ate 5 didn't drink

5 1 They didn't ~~had~~ **have** a good time.
2 His birthday is ~~on~~ **in** March.
3 Last year I ~~go~~ **went** on holiday to London.
4 The class starts ~~on~~ **at** six o'clock.
5 I ate pizza and ~~drinked~~ **drank** juice.

10 Test yourself

Vocabulary

1 1 clean 2 do 3 make 4 do 5 makes

2 1 sixty-five euros
2 fifty pence
3 fifty dollars
4 one hundred and twenty-five pounds
5 eight euros and fifteen cents
6 six dollars

Grammar

3 1 Did you go out?
2 What did you do last night?
3 Was Sandra at the quiz?
4 Where was Carl on Sunday night?
5 Did they enjoy the party?

4 1 c 2 d 3 b 4 e 5 a

Functional language

5 1 Can I **pay** by credit card?
2 Where **are** the changing rooms?
3 How much **is** this?
4 I'm just **looking**, thanks.
5 Can **I** help you?
6 **It** is twenty pounds, thanks.

11 Test yourself

Vocabulary

1 1 drive 2 type 3 play 4 swim 5 dance

Grammar

2 1 I can't swim.
2 She can speak Thai.
3 Can you hear me?
4 What can you do?
5 We can't hear the teacher.

3 1 am watching 2 aren't listening
3 is running 4 are … talking
5 is starting

4 1 a 2 b 3 b 4 a 5 b

Functional language

5 1 d 2 b 3 a 4 e 5 c

12 Test yourself

Functional language

1 1 speak 2 isn't 3 call 4 take 5 tell

Vocabulary

2 1 send 2 happy 3 turn off 4 call 5 tired

Grammar

3 1 Are you going to go on holiday?
2 When are you going to travel?
3 Is he going to see his friends?
4 Are they going to do the shopping tomorrow?
5 What is she going to do tonight?

4 1 going to do
2 'm going to see
3 'm going to study
4 'm not going to study
5 're going to have

Writing answer key

1 Completing a form

Reading

1 1 Manchester, United Kingdom 2 Berlin 3 44 603 295 4565 4 Roberts

2 Translate the words into your language. Check with your teacher.

Language focus

4 My name is Frank Roberts and I'm from Manchester. I'm in the Hotel Star in Berlin, in Germany.

Writing

5 Give your answers. Check with your teacher.
Sample answer
Mr ☑ Mrs ☐ Ms ☐
Last name(s): Clandfield
First name: Lindsay
Address: 277 Hillcrest Ave.
City: Toronto
Country: Canada
Telephone number:
Home: 555 123 4567
Work: 555 143 5689
Mobile: –
Email: lindsay@straightforward.col
Name of hotel: Regent Hotel City: London
Single room ☑ Double room ☐

2 A paragraph about you

Reading

1 1 T 2 F (He's a taxi driver and a student.) 3 F (His mother is from the US.) 4 T 5 F (His wife is from Germany.) 6 T

Language focus

3 1 What's your name?
2 My wife's name is **J**enny.
3 She's from **G**ermany.
4 Her parents are teachers. They're **G**erman teachers.
5 Their classes are on Tuesday and Thursday.

Writing

4 Give your answers. Check with your teacher.
Sample answer
My name's Lucas. I'm from Spain. My father is from Madrid and my mother is from Seville. I'm a student at Seville University. My English class is on Monday.

3 A person you know

Reading

1 1 sister 2 school 3 Russia 4 doesn't 5 week

Language focus

2 1 and 2 but 3 and 4 but

3 1 and 2 but

Writing

4 Give your answers. Check with your teacher.
Sample answer
My brother's name is Will. Will is 32 years old. He works with computers. Will is from Canada. He likes music and Italian food. He plays football in his free time.

4 A city description

Reading

1 1 Eight hundred thousand (800,000).
2 Yes, there are (two big parks).
3 The Golden Gate Bridge.
4 Chinatown.

Language focus

3 a M b M c E d S e M

4 1 d 2 b 3 a 4 e 5 c

Writing

5 Give your answers. Check with your teacher.
Sample answer
Budapest is a big city in Hungary. It is the capital city and has a population of 1,700,00. There are three big parks and eight bridges. It is a beautiful city.

5 A holiday blog

Reading

1 1 Marrakech. 2 A (beautiful) teapot. 3 In a café. 4 She went to the main square (and listened to the music).

Language focus

3 1 First 2 Then 3 first 4 then

Writing

4 Give your answers. Check with your teacher.
Sample answer
My holiday in Istanbul was fantastic. I arrived on Sunday. First I went to my hotel. Then I went shopping in the market. In the evening we went for a walk first, then we ate a meal in a restaurant. It was a nice day.

6 A letter asking for information

Reading

1 1 B 2 C

Language focus

2 1 Dear 2 or 3 am 4 about 5 like 6 more 7 about 8 Yours

Writing

3 Give your answers. Check with your teacher.
Sample answer
Dear Sir or Madam,
I am writing about your advertisement for the English Language course summer special. I would like more information about the dates and the price, please. Could you give me more details about the location?
Yours faithfully,
Arnold Lane